DUMBIN DOWN

Reflections on the Mis-Education of the Negro

JEFF MENZISE, PH.D.
FOREWORD BY
RAYMOND A. WINBUSH, PH.D.

Mind on the Matter
Publishing
P.O. Box 755
College Park, MD
20741
mindonthematter.com

10 9 8 7 6 5 4 3

Cover Design by Jeffery Menzise and Jerome Thompson.

Library of Congress Cataloging-in-Publication Data
Menzise, Jeffery,
        Dumbin' Down: Reflections on the Mis-Education of
        the Negro/ by Jeffery Menzise
includes Cover Artwork & Design, and Foreword by Raymond
A. Winbush.

ISBN 978-0-9856657-8-4

Pubished in 2012 by
Mind on the Matter Publishing,
P.O. Box 755, College Park, MD 20741
Website: www.mindonthematter.com
Email: drjeff@mindonthematter.com
240-988-9639

ACKNOWLEDGEMENTS

I want to thank all who made this project possible.
I am grateful to my family,
teachers, friends, mentors and
supporters. I am also appreciative to all those who have
contributed to this final product:
Morgan State University, Howard University,
Fisk University, Alkebu-lan Images and Books (Nashville),
Maati for her patience and assistance editing,
& my children for their constant inspiration.
A special thank you to my Ancestors, Orisha,
Guardian Spirits, and Spiritual Teachers/Initiators.

DEDICATION

This book is dedicated to all educators and
truth seekers, parents and children, journeying souls and
truth bringers.

"A critical work that reminds us that Carter G. Woodson's analysis remains relevant. Menzise has produced an informative guide for teachers, parents, school administrators, community organizers and others who care about the effective socialization of school-aged children."

Nefertari Patricia Hilliard-Nunn, Ph.D.
Lecturer, African American Studies
University of Florida

TABLE OF CONTENTS

FOREWORD

When Carter G. Woodson published "The Mis-education of the Negro" in 1933, little did he know that his reviving the use of the second word in his title from the 1620s, would survive to be used in the name of one of *the great recordings of all time (*The Mis-education of Lauryn Hill), in blogs, by politicians to describe poor education, video game enthusiasts, and filmmakers. He popularized a word that is now mainstreamed to describe any form of deliberately abusive "educational" training that distorts the worldviews of those who are victims of it. Thus, while Hill's recording describes the roadblocks and solutions faced by African American women in a racist and sexist society, it echoes Woodson's central theme of how African American people are deliberately propagandized to unlearn their African self and to imbibe large doses of white supremacy in all that they do.

Woodson's views of educating African people though written nearly 80 years ago, previsions in understanding what is going on with African people throughout the global system of white supremacy. The sameness of what Black children experience in their education — denigration, expulsion and marginalization — can be found in the barrios of East Los Angeles, the East Side of London, the Northwest Territories of Australia and the West Side of Baltimore. This sameness of mis-educating Black children and by default, Black people in general is no accident as Woodson says in Mis-education. Indeed it is deliberate, predictable and expected from a system of white supremacy that seeks to aggressively expand itself in all of the "Nine Areas of People Activity" described by Mr. Neely Fuller, Jr.

Dr. Menzise's latest book seeks to revisit what Woodson said in 1933 and connect the dots from then to now on the insidious nature of white supremacy's poisonous influence on the education of African Americans. Like Woodson, he is unsparing in his critique of the system of racism that engulfs us all and takes dead aim on how the system works and what to do about it. Like Woodson and unlike many of today's educators, Menzise is unsparing in his analyses of the mis-education of African people. And again, like Woodson you will find yourself exclaiming, "Yes!" every page or two as you revisit with him admonitions and warnings that are as relevant today as they were when Woodson wrote them 79 years ago.

I love the fact that Dr. Menzise has looked at each of the chapters in Woodson's classic and shown how the ideas he outlined eight decades ago are still relevant today. Menzise's deconstruction of each chapter is a seamless presentation of Woodson's idea while simultaneously being a commentary on the state of education, as it exists for Africans today. This is the companion volume I have been waiting for to mine the educational gems that Woodson presents and making them directly applicable to the education of African children today. I have heard countless times speakers imploring their audiences to read *The Miseducation of the Negro* but never being able to provide a "workbook" if you please to accompany the volume. Now that can be done with Dr. Menzise's book.

Lastly, and on a personal note, I have known Jeff for nearly 20 years and I have seen his evolution from a freshman at Fisk University to a Research Associate with the Institute for Urban Research at Morgan State University. When I have had the pleasure of introducing him, I never fail to say that he is the only student I have taught at the bachelors, masters and doctoral level. He has become a meticulous researcher especially as it relates to the effective education of African children. *Dumbin' Down* not only presents Jeff's deep knowledge of Woodson's prophetic utterances about educating African people, but his remarkable ability to apply them to today and provide practical ways of implementing them in the classroom and beyond.

I am also very excited because Dr. Menzise is one of the foremost media critics I know especially in the world of hip hop; I have gone to Jeff on many occasions to get his opinion about videos, lyrics and films and he never fails to provide important insights into how white supremacist media eagerly helps in the "dumbing down" of African people. This book will be read not only by adults and professionals but by students and younger generations as well. It is rare to the point of nonexistence that books on educating Africans are read by *both* young and old, but *Dumbin' Down* is such a book. You will enjoy reading it and recommending it to others.

Raymond A. Winbush
Director, Institute for Urban Research
Morgan State University
Baltimore, Maryland
June 21, 2012

iii

Preface

"May My Tongue Not Make Me Enemies…"

Odu Otura Ika
Sacred Oracle of Ifa

As a student of life and one who has consulted and worked as a clinical and school psychologist (K-12) in various states and school settings, a professor at several HBCUs as well as with several ministries of education internationally, the author has come to notice that there is a similarity between the educational and socialization systems that exist abroad and those here in the United States. The author has come to recognize that there is a divine task at hand, a task that was taken up by many of our great and honored ancestors (Shepsu/Egun); a task that must be continued until a solution has been produced, tried, tested and proven to yield a result that can at least grant a semblance of justice in a system where "true" justice is viewed as an antithesis to its own progress.

One of our honored Shepsu in this regard is Dr. Carter G. Woodson. He has, with all sincerity addressed the issues of education, mis-education, and the impact of oppression on victims of racism/White supremacy (a category that includes both Whites and non-Whites, although the impact is different for each group). He detailed, almost 80 years ago, the impact

v

of such an experience on the education process of Africans throughout the Diaspora, and has proposed viable solutions to the same. In his original work, published in 1933, Dr. Woodson addressed education in all nine areas of people activity, as developed by Neely Fuller, Jr., including: Economics, Education, Entertainment, Labor, Law, Politics, Religion, Sex, and War (Counter War). He humbly admits that he himself has been a part of the mis-education process, as have all of us who endeavor to educate, and who have also been mis-educated, under the current systems throughout the world. Very few are capable of breaking free from the simulated reality that we are inundated with on a daily, or even an hourly basis. For others, the majority, time is linear, spirit is only a concept to be dealt with on Fridays, Saturdays, or Sundays, depending on your yoke (religious perspective), and only in superficial, allegorical, and non-practical methods.

The masses still believe that we are "only" human and that divinity in flesh left with the crucifixion of the initiate Jesus who attained his "God" consciousness. They still believe that indigenous people around the world and their concepts of life, God (NTR, Nature), Self, and others is pagan, heathenistic, and something to be avoided at all costs. The above is hereby entered into the record as evidence of the mis-education process and the reason behind much of the hardship experienced by the inhabitants of planet Earth, regardless of race, nationality, gender, religious orientation, and class.

One of Dr. Woodson's motivations for publishing *The Mis-education of the Negro* was to provide "a corrective for methods which have not produced satisfactory results." (p. ix) As an educator, Dr. Woodson experienced first hand how such methods were designed, primarily for the construction and maintenance of a paradigm which holds as its essential formula the power equation of White superior to non-White.

He challenged the racist and ignorant notion that non-Whites were rightfully placed at the mercy of Whites because the latter (Whites) had a superior intellect and were acting in a charitable fashion by assisting the uncivilized and inferior African. Woodson championed the notion that the lifestyle of non-Whites during and after enslavement and colonization, is a lifestyle that was forced upon them, and that this imposed set of thought, speech, and actions are more a reflection of the enslavers, their society and its ruling class, than that of the one being forced to manifest the observed behaviors. The ability to survive, and in some instances thrive, under wickedly hostile conditions and produce great thinkers and doers such as Dr. Carter G. Woodson speaks volumes to the perseverance, resiliency, and sense of purpose deeply implanted and thoroughly permeating the being of those who once called divine-freedom their way of life.

Dr. Woodson made a profound and certain distinction between the mere imparting of information and actual education; the method of the three R's: Receive, Remember, Regurgitate, as opposed to Observe, Analyze, Think, Synthesize, and Build. He also notes that education "must result in making a man think and do for himself just as the Jews have done in spite of universal persecution." (p. x) He cautions one against citing isolated instances wherein it may "appear" that non-Whites have progressed beyond their oppressed identities (i.e., number of degrees conferred, number of non-White professionals, number of non-White millionaires, number of non-White firsts).

He unapologetically states that "if they are of the wrong kind the increase in numbers will be a disadvantage rather than an advantage." (p. xi) Meaning if these professionals are self-hating and consciously or unconsciously wedded to the White supremacist notion that non-Whites are inferior, then they will potentially be more destructive than the White supremacists themselves. Woodson continues by checking our emotional celebration of "achievement," in order to get a true sense of how capable the "successful and educated" non-White is at resisting oppression (psychological and material) as well as the likelihood that they will contribute to the maintenance, refinement and expansion of racism/White supremacy.

He further challenges his reader by pointing out how oppressed individuals seek to see the world through imaginary lenses; painting a picture of what it should be, instead of what it is. This delusional perspective keeps an individual from dealing with the truth of the situation at hand and encourages those non-Whites who have "achieved" high levels of education to challenge any perspective that opposes the status quo. Woodson believed this fear and reluctance on the part of the "accomplished" or "highly educated Negro" to be a residual effect of the plantation experience and the ongoing oppression of non-Whites at the will of White supremacy (Post Traumatic Slave Syndrome). He notes that it becomes second nature for non-Whites, who have themselves been disenfranchised for so long, to fear "anything that sounds like discrimination…[t]hey are anxious to have everything the White man has even if it is harmful." (p. xi)

The lack of empowerment in the modern systems of education is troublesome for both Whites and non-Whites. It lacks the basic principles necessary for developing and cultivating holistic thinkers, solution and strength-based approaches to situations, and dual-hemispheric functioning in both teaching and learning styles. This method of schooling is at the core of the socialization process in the West and is greatly responsible for the numerous social and cognitive issues faced by school-aged children today.

Throughout the establishment of the "New World," the great leaders of the West directly or indirectly sanctioned murder, rape, theft, terror, torture, peonage, segregation, deception and lynching. They outwardly dealt in psychotic behaviors while simultaneously pathologizing any attempt to be free by the oppressed (i.e., the invention of the psychological disorder drapetomania). The dichotomy of the modern system is perhaps its greatest flaw. While promoting the superiority of one race, it by default, and perhaps by design stamps the other races inferior; by highlighting only the modern era as making significant contributions to the progress of humanity, education neglects the millennia of yesterday when African nations and other non-White peoples successfully ruled and governed themselves. People educated by such a system become "a hopeless liability of the race." (p. xiii) This liability has far reaching implications and plays out in many behaviors that are all too common amongst non-Whites in today's society.

The "education" that has been provided to non-Whites has the potential to dumb down and subtly implant a "chip" of resentment for oppressed populations, especially towards those of one's own racial group. This resentment will often lead one to eventually despise the resented population and create a behavior syndrome that "avoids at all costs" any association or interaction with those in question. Hence we have the situation where far too many American Africans feel that the grass is greener, air is fresher, ice is colder, and food from a White grocer is better, simply because the grocer is White, the freezer is white, the grass is in the yard of White homeowners, and the nostrils inhaling the air are on a White face.

Now, there are many cases where one finds the grass *is* greener, air *is* fresher, and the produce in grocery stores *is* of a higher quality than that found in certain American African communities. The question here is not of the competence or actions of the community within which the produce, air and grass is located, but of the racist system which by design will deliver the higher quality foods to a grocery store (of the same brand) in the White community while delivering the low quality, almost stale/rotten foods to the stores in the American African community; or neglectfully and intentionally pollute the air in impoverished and American African neighborhoods; or destroy all "green-space" (parks, and natural forests) in the American African communities. The deeper implications come when the so-called "educated" attribute these differences to the competency and overall value system of the community, as opposed to seeking the source within the system itself.

We can draw similar examples from many institutions that exist in both American African and White communities, i.e., schools and professional services (i.e., dentists, medical doctors, plumbing, carpentry, lawn care, beauty supply stores). In each of these institutions, mis-education via the dumbing down process has once again served to dispose of any confidence that one may find in the abilities of American African professionals and has served to increase the blind faith in that of Whites.

If you're White you're Alright, If you're Brown Stick Around, If you're Yellow, you're Mellow, If you're Black, Stay Back!

Due to the psychological association of God, holiness, cleanliness, and divinity with the color white and with the White race, and the complimentary and dichotomous association of all things bad and evil with the color black and with the non-White races, one finds it difficult to look at the shear facts of history, see things as they objectively are and then draw fact-based conclusions from their analysis. It becomes difficult for one to readily identify Christopher

Columbus as a thug who pillaged and plundered the human beings indigenous to the islands that he first conquered. It becomes increasingly difficult to recognize that the actions of the colonial powers as they ravaged African nations (i.e., King Leopold II) are in fact actions similar to the human-headed locusts described in the very Bible published by the British Empire in 1611 (King James Version). It makes it ever so hard for individuals to discern good from evil, right from wrong, honesty from deception, and truth from falsehood.

The dumbing down process, as a tool, has served mercilessly to establish, maintain, expand, and refine the current paradigm of White supremacy; leaving one to focus solely on non-White inferiority, totally out of context of the environment that spawned such a notion, and totally without regard to the institutions and minds that perpetually fertilize its continued growth and production. To do otherwise is a revolutionary act; an act that requires strength, courage and wisdom. Strength to carry the sometimes heavy knowledge of truth. Courage to unapologetically proclaim that truth, and wisdom to raise one's self beyond reproach in your day to day thought, speech and actions.

The process of dumbing down has also grown ever more sophisticated and has taken a technological turn. The effectiveness by which children of infinite potential are convinced that it is better to be a self-proclaimed and proud "nigger" is astonishing. The efficiency with which the mis-educated continue to feed themselves and their children poisons (literally via foods and drugs, figuratively through methods of raising and socializing) is suicidal, abusive and torturous. The time for playing has long past; the seriousness of the situation and nature of the threat is that of enslavement evolved. Do we wait and become runaways or do we resist and become freedom fighters that remain free?

The battle is not solely of the flesh (physical means), but for the minds and souls of those that would perish…hence, the need for mis-education and dumbing down.

* Author's Note: The chapter headings are structured with Dumbin' Down chapter names in **bold** print with Dr. Woodson's chapter names immediately beneath in *(parentheses, bold, and italicized)* print.

Chapter 1

Still in the Hot Seat
(The Seat of the Trouble)

*"...to handicap a student by teaching him that his black face
is a curse and that his struggle to change his condition is
hopeless is the worst sort of lynching. It kills one's aspirations
and dooms him to vagabondage and crime."*

Carter G. Woodson
The Mis-Education of the Negro

It is an outstanding notion to not only recognize but to
also verbalize one's disdain for the hypocrisy that exists
within educational institutions amongst American Africans.
Yet Woodson did it. Furthermore, he dared to challenge the
"accomplishments" of the direct descendants of enslaved
Africans, which was risky business especially at a time when
such accomplishments were actively and conscientiously being
celebrated as "firsts." This celebration occurred with intense
emotion, and was carried out by the one's achieving (including
their families, friends and ancestors who fought to have the
right to progress beyond the plantation), and watched carefully
by those who designed the path by which such a person could
"achieve." This latter group had as their vested interest, the
total mis-education, misdirection, and confusion of the newly
"freed" African in order that they, the former enslaver, may
maintain their superior status and decrease the risk of it ever
being challenged. The methodology was simple yet effective.

History as a tool builds and constructs paths into the future. It simultaneously provides and works upon whatever materials are available in order to construct individuals, their personalities, their possibilities, their access to power, their perspective of self and others, as well as their basic and core values. With this in mind, it is easy to recognize the power involved in translating, transmitting, and transferring knowledge of history from one generation to the next and why so much intentional effort has been directed towards preventing the enslaved and newly emancipated Africans from carrying on such duties. Additionally, the information is skewed and configured in such a way that it now reflects a somehow inherent ignorance in the American African race, making this group seem beyond assistance and hope.

In American institutions of education, both predominately Black and predominately White, in 1933 and in 2012, many students are taught about their history from the perspective of those who have the most to lose if the truth is revealed. In other words, Christopher Columbus is still revered as an honest explorer who made friends with the "primitive" people he encountered in some strange land called Western India (hence the West Indies). King Leopold II is honored as a great monarch of Belgium who introduced abundant amounts of resources to the rubber industry, and the pilgrims as a group of good natured, god-fearing settlers who were fleeing unjust challenges to their freedom.

"Until Lions have Historians, the Story will ALWAYS Glorify the Hunter!"

How would these honored and revered individuals be labeled differently by those who suffered most from their presence? Christopher Columbus would become a pirate who raped, pillaged, stole and captured a group of innocent people who existed within their own concept of life (worldview). King Leopold II would become an individual who dealt a death blow to the continent of Africa in order to usurp its resources by force; visiting heinous acts of violence (including mutilation, torture, enslavement and murder) onto an innocent people. And of course the pilgrims, who were in actuality a group of criminals who came to the "new world" in order to escape persecution in their land, and brought with them disease and habits similar to those of the human-headed locusts of the Book of Revelations. They spread disease, attacked and stole land from the indigenous Americans, and served as one of the first dominoes in a line that would eventually end in the near extinction of all of the early American civilizations and peoples.

This is the side of the story that is withheld, or suspended in rhetoric and even "scholarly" debates, yet, it is rarely substantiated and justified, at an institutional level, with the facts that support and serves as evidence to its truth. Instead, individuals that champion the need for such truths to be held first and foremost, above and before any and all opinions, rationalizations, and defensive attempts to misinform and mis-educate, are often seen as "rabble-rousers" and individuals talking that "black stuff." In Dr. Woodson's day, to study and uphold such a perspective of history was considered a waste of time. More than three-quarters of a century later there remains the idea that to focus on and to bring these issues to light, is a futile attempt to replace racism with reverse racism.

The fact that history classes and departments, on the primary, secondary and post-secondary levels, continue to utilize textbooks and other "teaching" tools that reinforce the notions of the inferiority of non-White individuals and cultures, despite the fact that textbooks and other materials exist which tells a story that more closely represents the truth, speaks volumes to the intentional and continued racist deception via education. Why is it necessary to drill the thought of inferiority into the non-White "in almost every class he enters and in almost every book he studies?" (p. 2) And why is it that Dr. Woodson would feel that a child may be of better service to his people, as an adult, if "he happens to leave school after he masters the fundamentals, before he finishes high school or reaches college…?" (p. 2) Is it because the child would receive less of the lies that are often drilled into their impressionable minds? Would such a person have a better chance of contributing to their village in a positive, empowering and beneficial manner?

Perhaps it is because he felt that the highly educated "Negro" was not able to contribute to the constructive development of the remainder of the race, due to their thorough indoctrination into the belief system of their oppressors. This belief system would establish a dynamic which demands that the educated Black look down upon and be ashamed of the masses of his close and distant relatives. Sadly, the highly educated is often educated away from, both mentally and physically, their true culture and no longer understand the needs of their people, but have grown to focus more on the needs of society as a whole; in other words, the needs of the dominant culture; in other words, the needs of Whites.

This is similar to the forced and reckless abandonment experienced by the children of enslaved African women who had to breast feed the children of the enslavers, helping them to grow into productive and nurtured citizens. The African children, who would have enjoyed the touch, nurturing sustenance, and caring embrace while suckling at their mother's breast, suffered due to their parent's forced preoccupation with the well being of Whites. Perhaps the most

4

damaging aspect of this rejection was the lack of validation that comes from a mother and the adults in the village, who are willing to literally give of their own substance to sustain and nurture the next generation of oppressors. These children were and are left alone to try to understand how to negotiate a world wherein their basic needs were secondary, if not tertiary, to those of an unjust people and their oppressive system.

Spike Lee offered a solution to this phenomenon in his not so celebrated "joint" entitled "*The D.R.O.P. Squad.*" He directed a plot in which misled and mis-educated "Negroes" were literally "D.R.O.P.'d"; that is, they went through the process of "Deprogramming" for the sake of the "Restoration Of Pride." The movie's s/heroes were a band of doers who desired to correct the ills of dumbing down, psychological programming and mis-education by literally removing the "bad seed" from society, upon the request of a loved one or a concerned community member. Once removed, the target would be ushered through a process designed to systematically erase the false beliefs and challenge the deleterious actions, and replace them with notions of "Black Power" and "Black Pride." The end result, or at least the one hoped for, was to systematically cleanse the mind and spirits of the American African community in order to produce individuals who contributed to the upliftment and empowerment of the race.

This phenomenon is what Dr. Woodson considered to be "the seat of the trouble." He stated:

> Our most widely known scholars have been trained in universities outside of the South. Northern and Western institutions, however, have had no time to deal with matters which concern the Negro especially. They must direct their attention to the problems of the majority of their constituents, and too often they have stimulated their prejudices by referring to the Negro as unworthy of consideration.
> (p. 3)

He continues by citing the fact that much of the curricula at these universities, and even early aspects of education, are developed in their practical aspects without information, references, and models to directly address the situation of the oppressed American African populations. Even down to the religion and philosophy courses, American Africans were given misinformation and in many cases a conflicting set of rules, notions, and concepts that served more as propaganda and tools of misdirection, than as tools for empowerment and mental liberation, which ultimately amounted to an extreme waste of time.

In today's household, many inner-city American African youth do not actively participate in and/or experience discussions regarding family economics, the planning of family projects, or contribute and benefit from open discussions of the family's philosophical positions. Instead, many, as did those of Woodson's era, live in a basic survival mode, witnessing their parent(s) moving from job to job, hustle to hustle, plantation to plantation, looking for economic freedom they have never seen and have yet to experience. On the other hand, children of White families may enjoy the language of IRAs, stock market trends, bank accounts that draw interest, family assets, grand dad's will, the family business, and their bright future.

Unfortunately the situation has changed little. As Woodson highlighted in 1933, many American African children still attend schools that are in questionable physical condition, have scarce and substandard resources, and have instructors who may or may not be "certified" to teach and are perhaps "certifiably" crazy. These instructors often lack the sense of dedication and the self knowledge, wisdom and understanding necessary to prepare tomorrow's leaders for the task they must face. Hence, they prepare them to become batteries for the machine, giving of their time and life force to institutions that

contrast

are designed to limit opportunities and restrict freedoms.

Perhaps the most damaging form of this mis-education is with those 'bright minds" who enroll in divinity schools. They are still taught "the interpretation of the Bible worked out by those who have justified segregation and winked at the economic debasement of the Negro sometimes almost to the point of starvation." (p. 4-5) The internalization of such messages allows one to rule the masses in their congregations through manipulation and deception (both intentional and unconsciously), glorifying the "divine plan" of maintaining a status of cursed Hamites and born sinners, while Liberation Theology, as heralded by Rev. Jeremiah Wright is labeled as the gospel of hatred. There was a time when enslaved Africans were able to use the philosophical and spiritual underpinnings of Christianity to their advantage; taking the raw concepts, without the extra academic indoctrinations (because many were illiterate in regards to the standard English language), and applying them to their still vibrant and innate African spiritual consciousness, thus being made free by the dynamics of truth.

> "To manipulate history is to manipulate consciousness; to manipulate consciousness is to manipulate possibilities; to manipulate possibilities is to manipulate power."
>
> Amos Wilson
> The Falsification of Afrikan Consciousness

Throughout the Caribbean, South American nations, and in the south and southern coastal portions of the United States, one is able to identify the use of African Spiritual Sciences as a catalyst for the expression of Christianity. These men and women maintained their understanding of the power of their Gods and their Way. They also understood the necessity of the "double consciousness" and its instrumental role in their survival. Unfortunately, this was not taught in the institutions of higher education, nor was it validated by the religious vanguard. In fact, it was directly opposed by the use of terror, disassociation by the conjuring of fear, the deceptive use and interpretation of the "Wrath of God," and his strangely human-like quality of jealously. This fear factor was instilled and imposed upon the African with such precision that one would literally read "the word," and still accept images and concepts that directly contradict and conflict with the message.

One very clear example is with the color of Jesus and the other prophets, angels and holy men and women of the Old and New Testament. Modern images maintain the lie that "All that is White is Right," and "All that is Right is White." Solomon is black but comely; however, the popular pictures found in typical illustrated bibles make him appear to be European. Jesus hides in KMT (Egypt), and is stated to have hair like wool and skin like burned brass, yet he is visually depicted as a European. Joseph was mistaken to be an African (Egyptian), however, he too is commonly depicted as an individual of European descent. Moses, an African born (Egyptian) high priest and prince, is also visually portrayed as a European. Even in the case of leprosy turning a hand white, we still believed that dark skin is the curse.

What is it about the trained preacher that forces them to ask "Why does the color of Jesus matter?" when asked to interpret the facts? Why is it that highly educated American Africans tend to avoid the discussion regarding the brutal use of Christianity in the enslavement and continued oppression of the African throughout the Diaspora? How is it that we have not progressively and successfully challenged the utilization of education as a tool of further oppression, which sentences the deceived youth to a life of "vagabondage and crime?" Dr. Woodson made these statements almost 80 years ago. What is the current state of African youth on the planet? Here in the United States, American African youth, not all of them of course, but far too many are being primed and prepared for professional careers as criminals, inmates of greater confinement (prison), or mis-educated "leaders" to assist with the continued maintenance, expansion and refinement of the current system of injustice.

Woodson notices that:

> It is strange, then, that the friends of the truth and promoters of freedom have not risen up against the present propaganda in the schools and crushed it. This crusade is much more important than the anti-lynching movement, because there would be no lynching if it did not start in the schoolroom. Why not exploit, enslave, or exterminate a class that everybody is taught to regard as inferior?
>
> (p. 3)

He states that these "friends" have actually been equipped and prepared to live their lives as Europeanized and Americanized White men, and their true hope and desire is to convert and remake the African into their image; that is, the image of a confused individual with non-beneficial and non-empowering goals and objectives for self and their racial community. There is an actual aversion to the discussion of anything of race consciousness and a resistance to validate and/or support anything with the words "Black," "African," "Afrikan," etc., especially when linked to action verbs and adverbs such as "empowerment," "liberation," and "consciousness." They much more prefer the notion of simply being "American," or "children of God," which are great labels inasmuch as their definitions include justice in regards to the treatment of people.

The quandary appears once the "highly educated" realizes that he must be what Woodson calls "bisocial." He states that

While he is a part of the body politic, he is in addition to this a member of a particular race to which he must restrict himself in all matters social. While serving his country he must serve within a special group. While being a good American, he must above all things be a 'good Negro'; and to perform this definite function he must learn to stay in a 'Negro's place.' (p. 6)

This similar theme of mis-education is carried across various academic disciplines and permeates all nine areas of people activity (economics, education, entertainment, labor, law, politics, religion, sex, and war/counter-war). It is truly "the seat of the trouble." Unfortunately, little has been done in the past 79 years to change the aspirations of the "highly educated" American African from one of imitation of that which is perceived to be most successful (the model of Westernized institutions, thought processes and behavior constructs), to the more healthy and natural (for the African descendant) worldview of maintaining a value system which holds interpersonal relationships as supreme; a perspective that acknowledges the spiritual and material at once (as opposed to a materialistic focus); one that understands the necessity of dynamic differences and the value of all positions and roles in life (no longer belittling the tasks that have been labeled physical labor or blue collar).

Due to our collective confusion, which is directly related to the "death blow" to our divine consciousness dealt by the Ruffians (as discussed in Masonic lore), we have fallen into a death like state of being in which we have all but become zombies, batteries, and ventriloquist dolls to the master puppeteers. We have proudly taken our positions in the hot seat; valiantly defending our right to be ignorant of our circumstances and the reality of the situation, thus, we deny any need for action contrary to those currently making us "successful" in life. We have mistaken the flames of hell for the warmth of comfort. Parents now join the teachers in their belittlement of tomorrow's leaders; dealing low expectation and proud ignorance to the receptive minds of our children who rightfully, live up (or down) to these directives and become a dream yet deferred. There should be little question about how we ended up so far off target, yet, Woodson's next chapter, *How We Missed the Mark*, provides excellent points for reflection on the matter.

Dumbin' Down

Chapter 2

Locked and Loaded
(How We Missed the Mark)

"...mama forgive me, I should be thinkin bout Harvard, but that's too far away, niggaz is starving, nothing wrong with my aim just gotta change the target."

Jay-Z
American Dreamin

In the opening lines of Dr. Woodson's second chapter, he discusses how to truly understand the education of the post-enslavement African in America, by studying what he calls "the forces effective in the development of Negro education" (p. 9). These forces are the psycho-social, emotional, political and physical motivation for the liberation of the formerly enslaved Africans and the victimized reaction of the southern Whites, many of which were former wardens and property owners of their human chattel. This is consistent with the power equation of White supremacy (White over non-White), wherein it is necessary to maintain superiority over all those labeled inferior, and to refine, as well as expand, upon the systematic approach to successfully establish the concept as a reality.

When one reviews the founding of the nation's Historically Black Colleges and Universities (HBCUs), one will readily recognize that many were/are named after war generals and even those who are suspect White supremacists. The majority of these early universities were supported financially, politically, and academically by philanthropic Quakers and other White peoples, societies, and organizations. Is it possible for a conditioned oppressor to justly empower, through education, a race of people formerly and formally held to be domesticated farm chattel? At first glance it may seem possible, however, if one considers that enslaved Africans were most beneficial to their enslavers by being trained for specific roles, as opposed to being educated for the development and reclamation of their culture as free humans, then the possibility seems a little unlikely.

Woodson's prophetic vision and his understanding of the mis-education process is timeless and as accurate as degrees drawn with the Mason's square and compasses or the alignment of the temples and pyramids in the Nile Valley. Using the science of Sankofa, one is capable of identifying the embryo that existed in the experiences of yesterday, which inevitably became the wayward teenagers of today. This embryo, nurtured by the apparent well-wishers in the form of the Freedmen's Bureau and other Abolitionist successors, had as its genetic mission: the training of the former slave to maintain its inferior, submissive, and receptive-to-command status; and to, at all costs, deter them from thinking and developing a higher sense of self, culture, and to definitely prevent the development of a lucid understanding of their past and continued oppression. The mistake of the oppressive engineers was the assumption that education was the only means through which the formerly enslaved Africans could achieve beyond their oppressed status. This is a strong example of their Western epistemology, that is, a reflection of their notion of things only being known if it is perceived by the physical senses and is able to be duplicated through the scientific method.

These engineers seem to have neglected or ascribed to chance the record of the numerous empowered actions of the Ancestor's of the enslaved African. They have arrogantly and perhaps ignorantly refused to acknowledge the inherent intelligence and innate source of knowledge, wisdom, understanding, and practical application of the same; all of which had been demonstrated if by no other evidence than the fact that these people stood before them, after enduring the heinous and brutal experience of enslavement and cultural genocide, through their application of ingenious adaptations.

Nevertheless, there were great debates and a number of theories and hypotheses to surface regarding the most appropriate methods for educating the now impoverished American African who, via emancipation, found themselves in perhaps a more peculiar economic situation than when they were in physical bondage; much like the emancipated felon of today. This along with the social, political and psychological state of the American African made it necessary for the architects of "freedmen's education" to make certain unique provisions for this new group. Woodson noted that even these modifications and considerations were inadequately placed. He maintains that the well-wishers were, in fact, wishing to manifest a society that at the time, and some may argue presently, did not exist beyond their imaginations. The educational processes drafted for the freedmen did little to prepare the recently emancipated for reality, that is, the situation in which they were struggling to survive.

Of the newly emancipated African, Woodson reveals that "he was spending his time studying about the things which had been or might be, but he was learning little to help him to do better the tasks at hand." (p. 11) And thus, pervasive stagnation was the order of the day, wherein the newly emancipated people were herded like cattle to the fields to graze, then returned immediately to their stalls. It's the proverbial carrot dangling in front of the donkey to keep them hopeful enough to continue walking.

As highlighted by Woodson, even our modern education processes do very little to assist the American African to deal with their present circumstances. The current system does very little to assist with the empowerment of American Africans; it does very little to break the psychological chains of slavery in order that the ex-slave may once and for all rise beyond the brutally implanted notions of inferiority; it is an ineffective tool for rekindling, within the American African, that flame that draws toward itself "light," in order that their melanin may once again take on its superior function amongst the many living substances of the human being. Conversely, many of the modern tools for education are diametrically opposed to revealing the truth regarding the American African's ancestral contributions to the creation of modern greatness.

It is very interesting that many American Africans are taught to believe in the God "I Was" and the God "I Will Be" and rarely in the God "I Am." Meaning that emphasis is placed on the biblical (Old and New Testament) versions of God; a God that once blessed, died, and promises to be resurrected to correct the wrongs that take place during "His" absence. This teaching flies in the face of traditional Wisdom concerning the three main attributes of God: Omniscience (All Knowing), Omnipresent (In All Ways Present), and Omnipotent (All Powerful). By perpetuating the time-limited concept of God, the teachers and champions of this doctrine disarm and ill-equip their subjects for spiritually dealing with the present time in any real or practical manner. The same goes for the separation of God from wo/man by externalizing the Divine Presence and placing It in the sky.

Woodson further elaborates on his point by highlighting the response of the State and City level educational authorities, to the notion of repatriation to Africa; not only did they begin to shift the curriculum, but also enlisted many American Africans to carry on the debate within their own communities:

> For a generation thereafter the quarrel as to whether the Negro should be given a classical or practical education was the dominant topic in Negro schools and churches throughout the United States. Labor was the most important thing of life, it was argued; practical education counted in reaching that end; and the Negro worker must be taught to solve this problem of efficiency before directing attention to other things…The schools in which they were educated could not provide for all the experience with machinery which White apprentices trained in factories had. Such industrial education as these Negroes received, then, was merely to master a technique already discarded in progressive centres…except what value such training might have in the development of the mind by making practical applications of mathematics and science, then, it was a failure. (p. 11 - 12)

This level of distraction and pacification of the vital, self-determining energy is utilized again and again from the time of Dr. Woodson's original writing to the time of this reflection. It is apparent that even 'til now, the American African has never, en mass, reclaimed their horticultural, psycho-spiritual, and theological knowledge; this would be the most practical and efficacious education that one could possibly possess under the current and past circumstances of a similar nature. How did we miss the target? Fear. The fear that was introduced into the lineage of Africans during the Americanization of their culture is probably one of the most understudied and ill-addressed variables contributing to the current status of the race as a whole.

There are countless numbers of situations wherein an advocate of truth sought to challenge, on behalf of American

17

Africans, the ongoing perpetuation of falsehoods, injustice, and oppressive systems only to be incarcerated, assassinated, or so well intimidated that they were rendered ineffective to champion their self-proclaimed cause. Many of these people have and continue to sacrifice (give up something that may be more desirable) in order to shine light onto the shadows of deception. Why would these attempts to promote empowerment of American Africans through correct self-knowledge be challenged and met with such brutality? Why so much misdirection and deception? Why is it so important for master marksmen to take aim at the wrong targets?

The brutality and intentional misdirection and deception are there to keep the focus of the oppressed on targets that serve to maintain their oppression, or will do little to effect any true change to their oppressive situation. Paradoxically, these targets are the ones with the greatest and highest reward when one successfully strikes it. For example, right now in the world of pop culture the greatest rewards (money, fame, respect) are given to those who promote ignorance and criminal behaviors (i.e., self identification with the personality of a nigger, violence, drug dealing, etc.), non-productive concepts (vanity and arrogance) and magnified consumerism. The promotion and marketing of this culture is phenomenal and often carries a very expensive price tag, and packs stadiums, arenas, and concert halls. While those scholars who attempt to pack a lecture hall for the deliverance of positive "rap" in the form of lectures and workshops, often speak to more chairs than people.

Sad reality [handwritten margin note]

To further concretize the notions of inherent ignorance, many global systems of education continue to consider and teach that Africa has no greatness and that the Nile Valley is an Oriental designation. In addition to this illogical and deceitful concept, many also entertain theories which contribute the construction of the continent's vast and wondrous monuments to space creatures, and its high level of civilization and culture to foreign invaders. These lies and non-productive debates persist in spite of the evidence. No conclusion is ever reached amongst the "scientific" community and room is always left for debate; this allows for the continuation of confusion and the practice of rhetoric.

In the primary and secondary school environment, children are taught from non-practical curricula which deemphasize the need for self-sufficiency, productivity, and the ability to provide for one's self, the basic needs of food, clothing, and shelter. This is done either through neglect (intentional or unintentional), or through the direct and deliberate teaching of consumerism and dependency. In addition to this misdirection and deception, today's youthful generations are introduced to, and has its detrimental behaviors enforced by, images promoting destruction, death and violence as the most productive means of gaining "success" and basic fulfillment in life.

The impact and effectiveness of this message is easy to identify. Simply visit an elementary school (one that does not require the students to wear uniforms), and view how the children attempt, with the assistance of their parents, to imitate the fashions and behaviors advertised by their favorite hip hop artists. Unfortunately, this phenomenon is at an early stage of being introduced to this young audience; it is subsequently reinforced and carried throughout one's matriculation, from elementary to post secondary (college and professional schools). How does one muster up the courage to stand steadfast in the truth while engaging our future? At one point in African history, the truth (Maat) was held in high regard… what happened? How is it that the all important task of guiding and socializing our children and teaching them how to shoot for their goals was so easily co-opted and neglected? Why is the Truth no longer held in high regard by the masses? Dr. Woodson attempts to answer these questions in his next chapter *How We Drifted Away from the Truth*, which is the next chapter for reflection.

Chapter 3

...And the Truth Shall Make You FREE!
(How We Drifted Away From the Truth)

"The Truth is the Truth and that's no offense. Why fools don't know themselves. They think they've got the answer but really I don't know."

Buju Banton
The Truth

Woodson begins his third chapter with a most appropriate and truth driven question. He asks "How, then, did the education of the Negro take such a trend?" (p. 17) This question, in the "new millennium" is as relevant as ever. When we chart the progress of education from the pre-Civil War enslavement era to now, we should be honest and very clear that the word progress may be a misnomer. Education, in the truest aspects of the word, has not lived up to its definition which is: to bring out, awaken, develop and cultivate the natural talents held within an individual. Instead, there has been much cultivation of social class distinction, and a large demonstration of the willingness to disseminate both relevant and irrelevant information, as well as the willingness of the "needy" to devour and assimilate, with little discernment, the bones being thrown at their feet; all the while the true cultivation of thinking and self-actualized individuals is more than lacking.

From the Mississippi Law of 1832, which prevented the enslaved from being "educated" through threats of bodily harm, to the more recent "no child left behind campaign," the socialization offered through education has not consistently provided the "promised" empowerment and liberation to the masses of American Africans. Instead, as stated by Woodson, it has been "more of an effort toward social uplift than actual education. Their aim was to transform the Negroes, not to develop them." (p. 17) To comprehend this perspective is to gain important insight into the education question posed above. It identifies the main motivating factors and the intended direction towards which the American African would be steered by "education," like cattle on a ranch. To uplift the American African socially is highly ambiguous and could mean a multitude of things. Some would argue that the only social upliftment that occurred during this period of time was from being chattel, to working as indentured servants on the same plantation where they were once held captive. This routine placement of formerly enslaved Africans into socially packaged categories, that demand their compliance with a system designed to diminish their light, is a detestable and common form of psycho-sodomy.

Like the well wishers of yesterday, rarely is there an educator today who understands the monstrous task before them. The mainstream system of educating today's learner has been streamlined and converted into a factory-type situation, in which the educated are being mass-produced in assembly line fashion; producing high levels of academic apathy, social retardation, and fodder for the cannons aimed at themselves in a sort of suicidal gesture. The force fed curricula of yesterday, has now stepped up in its method of delivery, morphing into an intravenously delivered toxin; a toxin designed to perpetuate the propaganda and ill-gotten facts regarding the ancestral legacy of both White and non-White populations.

Dr. Woodson identified this phenomenon as the core factor in the cultivation of race hatred of the American African, by both Whites and American Africans themselves.

Can it be that it was all so simple? If Dr. Woodson is correct in his assessment, then it must mean that by correcting this atrocity called education, one should be able to solve what Mr. Neely Fuller, Jr. calls "the most important problem faced by humans living in the known universe," that is, the problem of racism/White supremacy. In other words: to eradicate modern Sambo, and to reintroduce the concept of divinity into the identity of those of African lineage should, hypothetically, produce a miracle. This miraculous reinstatement of inner justice and inner peace as a viable option for human existence is a natural by-product of proper training, socialization, and intentional identity development. This entire process will be facilitated by truth and education working hand in hand.

Dr. Woodson describes how the neglected and insufficient attention given to the African across academic subject is consistently reflected in the social sphere. He identified many such instances as they existed in 1933, however, he could have very well written this reflection as there is little to be changed, because so little has changed. There is still a "need" for a "special" time of year to celebrate and discuss the historical, scientific, and scholarly contributions made by continental and diasporic Africans. There is still a "need" for "special" courses that focus on the African and their contribution to world civilization and history. There is still a "need" for "special" sections in the library for African books written for, by, and/ or about African people. This, at first glance may be called progress, like a dagger pulled half-way out of the back of an unsuspecting victim; however, once re-spected (looked upon again), it is obvious that the individual is still in a serious and critical situation. This so-called progress serves as a pacifier for those who have a need to share their awareness of such Truths; it simultaneously serves as a subtle buffer for those who would rather not bother with such information. It carves out a special, contained place for the carrying on of such "trends and fashions."

In regards to the linguistic capabilities of Africans, we now know of the complexity and unity amongst the African tongues; for this we give special thanks to Drs. Diop, Obenga, Van Sertima, Smitherman, Beatty, Woods, etc. The power inherent in such knowledge is clear to the modern educator and researcher; what is less apparent is the fact that during the days of Europe's conquest of Africa, the deceitful missionaries were taught the formal use of these languages in order to exploit and manipulate their unsuspecting prey. The sophisticated nature of these languages is rarely publicly highlighted, and descendants of these cultures are often encouraged to forsake their Ancestral languages for that of their colonial and enslaving "masters." To this day, one would be hard pressed to find a well established African language course/program at one of over 100 Historically Black Colleges and Universities (HBCUs) in the U.S. (Howard and Tennessee State Univ. being two shining exceptions); the focus remains the same: no value is given to the underlying culture and contribution of those whose ancestry is traced to Africa. Unbelievably, there are still arguments made regarding the race of the Kamau of Ancient Kemet (Egypt)…a crime that separates complex systems of writing from the continent of Africa and her children.

In a powerful and little known documentary, "Black History, Lost, Stolen or Strayed," Dr. Cosby takes the viewer on a brief journey highlighting the contributions of Africans to modern culture. He shows how Picasso's art imitates West African sculptors and painters from ancient and modern times. He further demonstrates how the absence of positive representations of Africans in modern curricula, and/or the onslaught of negative portrayals, literally impacts the self-concept of American African children. He provides, as evidence, examples of a well known psychological assessment technique called "human figure drawings." Many of the American African children whose drawings were highlighted in the film displayed indications of low self-esteem and a negative self-concept. Conversely, the majority of the White children whose drawings were highlighted had clear indications of a healthy and empowered self-concept.

The prophetic Woodson furthers his chapter by identifying how American African law students were taught that the American African was the epitome and main perpetrator of criminal behavior. Although academically and politically supported by crime statistics (mostly incarceration rates by category), the truth behind criminal activity, criminal behavior, and the historical criminalizing of a race for economic and political purposes was rarely highlighted. This neglected information would potentially serve as the context for the proper interpretation of the aforementioned facts and stats.

This historical situation has laid the foundation for the current infatuation and lack of concern about criminality by large numbers of American Africans. For example, when we see that three-quarters of a century later, a young American African child chooses to most identify with those pop culture characters that promote criminal and maladaptive behaviors, and as a result, there is a preponderance of American Africans in greater confinement (incarcerated in prisons and jails), we must recognize this as a sustainable effort and that very little beneficial progress has been achieved. It was once stated in a lecture by Amos Wilson that "the more Black officers enlisted, the more Black people ended up in jail; the more Black psychologists, the more Black people went crazy." His intention was to identify how the superficial gaze of a weary American African might mistake the morphing of injustice into something more palatable, for true gain and progress. Mr. Neely Fuller, Jr. identifies this as the "refinement" phase of racism (White supremacy).

The insidious use of education as a tool for displacement of the African descendant within the known universe is appalling and seems to be cognitive genocide. The skillful use of history to permanently affix the status of Africans as inferior, pitiful, and expendable in regards to all other races on the planet, is the smoking gun clumsily dropped at the crime scene. There is no need for the infrared lights, ballistics, and forensic investigations; this one is elementary dear Watson. Woodson elaborates:

> An observer from the outside of the situation naturally inquires why the Negroes, many of whom serve their race as teachers, have not changed this program. These teachers, however, are powerless. Negroes have no control over their education and have little voice in their other affairs pertaining thereto. The education of Negroes, then, the most important thing in the uplift of the Negroes, is almost entirely in the hands of those who have enslaved them and now segregate them. (p. 22)

The number of HBCUs founded by, and named after Europeans bear witness to this notion (Howard, Fisk, Meharry, etc.). He continues:

> With "mis-educated Negroes" in control themselves, however, it is doubtful that the system would be very much different from what it is or that it would rapidly undergo change. The Negroes thus placed in charge would be the products of the same system and would show no more conception of the task at hand than do the Whites who have educated them and shaped their minds as they would have them function. Negro educators of today may have more sympathy and interest in the race than the Whites now exploiting Negro institutions as educators, but the former have no more vision than

their competitors. Taught from books of the same bias, trained by Caucasians of the same prejudices or by Negroes of enslaved minds, one generation of Negro teachers after another have served for no higher purpose than to do what they are told to do. In other words, a Negro teacher instructing Negro children is in many respects a White teacher thus engaged, for the program in each case is about the same. (p. 23)

And thus,

There can be no reasonable objection to the Negro's doing what the White man tells him to do, if the White man tells him to do what is right; but right is purely relative. The present system under the control of the Whites trains the Negro to be White and at the same time convinces him of the impropriety or the impossibility of his becoming White. It compels the Negro to become a good Negro for the performance of which his education is ill-suited. For the White man's exploitation of the Negro through economic restriction and segregation the present system is sound and will doubtless continue until this gives place to the saner policy of actual interracial cooperation-not the present farce of racial manipulation in which the Negro is a figurehead. History does not furnish a case of the elevation of a people by ignoring the thought and aspiration of the people thus served. This is slightly dangerous ground here, however, for the Negro's mind has been all but perfectly enslaved in that he has been trained to think what is desired of him. ***The "highly educated" Negroes do not like to hear anything uttered against this procedure because they make their living this way, and they feel that they must defend the system. Few mis-educated Negroes ever act otherwise; and, if they so express themselves, they are easily crushed by the large majority to the contrary so that the procession may move on without interruption [Emphasis added].*** (pp. 23-24)

This brilliant psycho-social analysis of the systematic processes directly responsible for the current state of education, in regards to American Africans, is clearly evidenced by the current conditions of HBCUs and their student populations. The academic performance, the textbooks used to teach, the perspective, mind-state, research interests and worldview of the individual instructors, as well as the distinct difference in treatment, compensation, and opportunities given to those who "go along with the program" are clear examples of the steady decline in these once "progressive" institutions. Those who seek to speak against the structural flaws making up the foundation of curricula used to "mis-educate" are more likely to be "corrected" than the corrupt administrations and governing boards of trustees whose apparent purpose is the systematic dismantling of the HBCU.

The need for educational reform has been the outcry by many regardless of race and class; however, an educational overhaul only makes sense if there is, in deed, a higher purpose for education in these United States. Unlike the developmental processes undertaken by ancient cultures and civilizations of the non-Western world of yesterday, today's system is driven by an axiological perspective that places the highest value in the acquisition of objects as opposed to harmonious interpersonal interactions between all that is created. This may, on the surface, appear to be a minor bone to pick, however, when one ponders the implications of this material driven value system the danger is at once made clear.

For example, choosing to place commodities, their production and consumption, above the overall wellbeing of people is the beginning of the deterioration of the moral standards of any society. Character development, which is highly valued in these societies, is driven by the desire to ensure harmony amongst its systems (human and otherwise). This cultural trait must take the back seat, especially if the basic necessities of life are to be maintained. The subtle deterioration is demonstrated by the innumerable acts of senseless violence exacted upon millions of Africans, indigenous Americans and other peoples of color, by those seeking to acquire materials for their own growth and development. It was taken as far as to literally objectify the people themselves, turning entire populations, for generations, into chattel slaves.

Perhaps the only "flaw" found by this author in Woodson's third chapter is the notion that one has simply "drifted" from the truth. A more accurate method of addressing the situation would be to ask "how were we deliberately steered from the truth?" The so-called "benign neglect" committed by those who Dr. Woodson speaks about in this chapter is in all actuality a deliberately developed scheme to not only leave out the African's many contributions to civilization, but to also leave out the heinous and inhumane acts of violence carried out by the European and their American descendants.

Interestingly, a few years ago the author was conducting a workshop on racism in a small town in the South during which an older White female who was also an educator and psychologist, courageously stood up to address the other Whites in attendance. She eloquently stated that the reason for the omission of the brutal acts visited upon Africans and other non-Whites by the hand of Whites, was to protect their [White] children from having to identify their [racial] group, and thus themselves, with such a horrible display of thought, speech, and action. And that they [Whites] have not only left out a particular perspective, but have in fact "left out the Truth." Another elder White lady continued by stating that it would not be the responsibility of American African educators to correct the lies, but the responsibility was with "those who look like me" [other Whites], because they are the one's with the power and they are the one's responsible for the current state of affairs.

If this is in fact the case, and if we are in fact riding on their [Whites'] vessel, then would the captain be so honorable as to go down with their ship? Will the band play on as in the

Titanic's last moments? Or will the mis-educated American African be standing at the helm, left to sink or swim and shoulder the responsibility of those who have thus despised them enough to create ignorance regarding their true role and rights in the situation? Either way, we should now place our scuba gear on and prepare to venture into a deeper analysis of the current situation by reflecting on Dr. Woodson's fourth chapter "*Education Under Outside Control*."

Chapter 4

Designated Schooling
(Education Under Outside Control)

"Negroes trained under such conditions without protest become downright cowards, and in life will continue as slaves in spite of their nominal emancipation."

Carter. G. Woodson
The Mis-education of the Negro

"We build their penitentiary. We build their school. They brainwash education, to make us the fool."

Bob Marley
Crazy Baldheads

Interestingly, Dr. Woodson starts his fourth chapter by acknowledging those Whites who have been instrumental in the uplift of American Africans. This approach was most likely to ensure that his honest and direct assessment and resulting criticism of those who are guilty of "educating" American Africans was not mistaken for blaming all Whites. He recognizes that there are several Whites who have contributed and sacrificed greatly to assist in the physical and mental emancipation of American Africans in spite of the danger of such actions.

In these more recent times, there have also been courageous Whites who have spoken out against racism/White supremacy,

White Privilege, and spoken out for equality, justice and the freedom of those suffering at the hands of systematic oppression and injustice. However, as stated by Dr. Woodson, there are many, many more that have treated shame with shamelessness, proudly waving the banner of White superiority and non-White inferiority. Some would even posit that those who do not simultaneously relinquish their "White-privilege" are only paying lip-service to the struggle for freedom, justice, and equality on behalf of American Africans, and are thus ineffective when it comes to establishing justice as "designated educators."

The analogy of the "designated driver" describes education under outside control by illustrating the profound dynamic embedded in this concept. Typically, the notion of a designated driver evokes thoughts of alcohol consumption, drunkenness, dependency, and dependability. In essence, one *needs* a designated driver due to some impairment, or condition, while simultaneously assuming that the designated driver has better judgment, and/or is more capable of successfully carrying out the designated task. In every case, the driven has directly or indirectly chosen to go wherever the driver drives. Again, the assumption is that the driven will be taken to a place that is safe, and of their own choosing or at least co-determined. In many respects, we have erroneously placed the same assumptions on the process of "designated educating," and are now suffering dearly for such a mistake.

Regarding the education of young children in the U.S., the appointment of designated educators is common practice. Many parents relinquish the role, responsibility, and honor of exposing children to life in a systematic and intentional way, with the purpose of producing a specific and desired outcome. Hence, their children are carrying forth someone else's value system, priorities, and perspective of reality. If there is congruence between the parents' and designated educator's desires, intents and purposes, and if these are healthy and constructive for the children, then outcomes are likely to be favorable. However, in the case where there is disagreement (consciously or not), then the well-being of the child and likelihood for beneficial outcomes is severely compromised. This assumes that the parents' desires for their children are for their best, and that of the designated educator is questionable, or vice versa. The key is to minimize conflicting worldviews by finding the most beneficial perspective for the child and seeking educators who will compliment and accommodate this in their craft.

Dr. Woodson speaks of how certain individuals are useless when it comes to educating American Africans. He cites their lack of spirit (good will) and their ineptitude when it comes to teaching in accredited institutions. He furthers by criticizing the American African institution of higher learning for not scrutinizing, to the degree of rejecting, some of these "unworthy" applicants. He laments that the HBCU is far too willing to accept White applicants based on their Whiteness while under-scrutinizing their credentials. The author has experienced the results of such a crime as a student, an administrator, and as a professor at an HBCU. For example, a White professor of psychology offered the author's classmate (an American African female) a frontal lobotomy as a solution for her poor performance on an exam. This professor was certifiably insane, yet, held a tenured position on the faculty at this prestigious HBCU. The author has also witnessed situations in which a less qualified White professor would receive promotions and pay increases over their more competent and accomplished American African colleagues.

It should be of no surprise then that the HBCU is in great decline and is the subject of much conversation, gossip, and drama. The institution seems to have lost its spirit and common survival instincts. It seems that for the period of time surrounding the era of "1st Black presidents," HBCUs were overtly carrying forward their mission of stabilizing the institution for the sake of longevity, transmission of an intellectual legacy to future generations, and the upliftment of character, skills and competencies of American Africans. Nowadays, while the mission remains the same on paper, the product (i.e., mis-educated students) reflects something all together different. Of course this is not applicable to every HBCU, but unfortunately, it can be applied to many.

At one time this author held a belief that educators, on the college level, were purposely producing incompetence. There seemed to have been this unspoken rule to excuse and accept the excuses brought to our emails, office hours, and telephones by students who for one reason or another failed to produce academically and subsequently received a failing grade. It is amazing how many professors would simply pass a student in order to avoid further drama; while others would at-least give an extra assignment to make up points missed. It's amazing how many professors would neglect their duty to engage their students in meaningful conversation and dialogue during class-time instruction, and instead, waste class-time reviewing the current events of that day; a task which is often rewarded with the label of "favorite teacher" amongst the slackers.

The implications of such "educating" practices are far reaching and impacts those who desire to maintain a standard of academic expectation that exceeds mediocrity. Those who deviate from the educational practices outlined above tend to have unfavorable reputations. In fact, a professor labeled as "difficult" or "hard" tends to be one who refuses to accept laziness, lack of effort, and disrespect (in the form of consistent tardiness, classroom disruption, sleeping, texting & web-surfing during instruction) as a normal experience in their classroom.

This professor tends to value education as a tool for increasing one's "lot" in life via cultural infusion and the development of a productive and self-respecting character. These are the women and men who deal in what Woodson calls "real education." Those who have been tenured may maintain this standard and continue to challenge their students to perform beyond their comfort zone, while those who are not tenured may, and often times do, collapse under the pressure applied by students conspiring to complain and shift the blame of their own academic failure to their professors' "inability to teach." It can be a catch 22 of sorts, especially when the "customer" (our students) are always right.

The complaining alone is not the issue, in fact, all things public and private are up for scrutiny. It is the institution's willingness and desire to avoid having their own lack of standards brought into question beyond closed-door meetings. This is what allows the undue and unjust pressure to be placed on those "real educators," coercing them to conform to substandard expectations. It becomes a sticky situation. The true educators can choose to: 1) hold their square and weather the storm as best they can, 2) jump-ship, or 3) compromise for the sake of maintaining their job. In the end, the students and the institution as a whole suffer.

There are certain HBCUs that maintain as department heads White individuals, which is not a problem, nor an issue because at the same time they also have American African department heads. The issue is when the leadership at these institutions maintain the lie that White is superior to non-White and unfairly appoint, promote and hire White academicians to fill their ranks, while overlooking American Africans who are equally or more qualified for the same position. Believe it or not, this problem occurs more than some would care to know and/or admit. It is a crushing experience to the educational outlook and reputation of the HBCU.

The above statements are a mere echo of what Woodson eloquently highlights when he states:

> To be frank, we must concede that there is no particular body of facts that Negro teachers can impart to children of their own race that may not be just as easily presented by persons of another race if they have the same attitude as Negro teachers; but in most cases tradition, race hate, segregation, and terrorism make such a thing impossible. The only thing to do in this case, then, is to deal with the situation as it is.

> Yet we should not take the position that a qualified White person should not teach in a Negro school. For certain work which temporarily some Whites may be able to do better than the Negroes there can be no objection to such service, but if the Negro is to be forced to live in the ghetto he can more easily develop out of it under his own leadership than under that which is super-imposed. The Negro will never be able to show all of his originality as long as his efforts are directed from without by those who socially proscribe him. Such 'friends' will unconsciously keep him in the ghetto. (p. 28)

This restriction of expression is one of the key factors in the "mental drop-outs" experienced by American African males in the 4th grade. Oft times, White teachers instructing non-White students are culturally incompetent, and fail to understand their own conscious and unconscious prejudices that color their instruction style and expectations for their students. The American African experience is becoming increasingly void of the "common sense schools and teachers who understand and continue in sympathy with those whom they instruct." (p. 28)

There are many articles published that highlight the impact of cultural competency, teacher expectations, relevant classroom instruction, etc. on student performance. There are also countless numbers of books, manuals, workshops, curricula, and systems designed to enhance academic performance and outcomes. So why is there still such a disparity in the implementation of updated educational "best practices" when it comes to educating predominately American African populations? Is it because education is maintained under outside control? Dr. Woodson thought so, and this author agrees. He states that:

> At least a hundred youths should wait daily upon the words of this scientist [George Washington Carver] to be able to pass on to the generations unborn his great knowledge of agricultural chemistry… In education itself the situation is the same. Neither Columbia nor Chicago can give an advanced course in Negro rural education, for their work in education is based primarily upon what they know of educational needs of the Whites. Such work for Negroes must be done under the direction of the trail blazers who are building school houses and reconstructing the educational program of those in the backwoods. Leaders of this type can supply the foundation upon which a university of realistic education may be established. (p. 36)

This sentiment, made modern, deals with the need for more home-based instruction; whether through the establishment of official home-schools, or the training of parents in child developmental processes and the educational skills needed to provide the solid foundation to build life skills, a love for learning, confidence, and a drive towards excellence. Of course the best answer is all inclusive, meaning both the need for parenting skills development and the establishment of more home-schooling programs are equally important and relevant, and are both viable options for solving the major issues facing American Africans in regards to education. Education under outside control is what promotes the very dichotomous (either/or) thinking purposely illustrated above.

This phenomenon is what encouraged the debates and arguments between W.E.B. Du Bois and Garvey, Booker T. Washington, etc. It's the same motivating force behind the left-brain oriented, rational and logic models that have been held as supreme when it comes to determining truth; it's what causes the denigration of indigenous cultures, their civilizations, epistemology and overall way of life; hence it simultaneously creates generations of accumulated biases and an educational paradigm based solely on the dominant culture's views, biases, mistakes, and gains.

Whole-brain learning is the key. It is what will eventually expand our conceptualization of self (including our human capabilities) beyond the limitations implanted by years of trauma, ignorance, oppression, and mis-education. People mistakenly thought that Du Bois' notion to enhance the intellectual capabilities was diametrically opposed to Washington's proposal to develop life skills and trades; the same way that people were led to believe that Malcolm X's notion of self-respect, self-defense, and self-sufficiency was in conflict with Dr. Martin Luther King's message of love and unity. The reality is that all of the above are necessary for one to truly *learn to make a living*, and to progress beyond their current situation and lot in life.

To strengthen one's reasoning abilities, analytical and synthesizing thought processes, while simultaneously learning how to grow food, use tools and master materials is/was the corner stone of any TRUE system of education (initiation) and the establishment of a healthy society. In Woodson's next chapter, he discussed the dangers associated with a society where the vast majority of its people failed to *learn to make a living*. You will find that his words are prophetic and that we, some 80 years later, are reaping the fruit from such a neglectful and misguided approach to education.

Chapter 5

Get up, Get Out, and Get Something
(The Failure to Learn to Make A Living)

*"Give a person a fish, and they will eat for a day; Teach a
person to fish, and they will eat forever."*
-Ancient Proverb

"A man who cuts his own wood warms himself twice."
**-Baba Boyce Brunson,
Son of Queen Mother Burnece Walker Brunson**

*"The thought of the immediate reward, shortsightedness, and
the lack of vision and courage to struggle and win the fight
made them failures to begin with."*
**-Carter G. Woodson
The Mis-education of the Negro**

Called the "first essential in civilization" by Dr. Woodson,
the ability to make a living is predicated upon being taught
to make a living. Many automatically assume that "making
a living" is strictly concerned with earning money to pay
the expenses of life. To the contrary, "to make a living"
encompasses far more than financial stability; it also includes:
overall resourcefulness, character development, pro-social
personalities, adaptability, and basic survival skills (including
self-defense) that are designed to enhance and preserve a
certain quality of life. American Africans through enslavement,

post-emancipation and modern times, have consistently been taught to develop a certain level of dependency on people, systems, and things outside of themselves, which are often diametrically opposed to their well-being. For example, while on the plantation enslaved Africans were taught (directly and indirectly) that their survival was based on the whims of the plantation owner and their (the plantation owner's) psychotic temperament. Post emancipation, American Africans were released from the physical shackles, yet maintained in a state of psychological and economical dependency for things as "basic" as human rights, food, clothing, and shelter. Once the American African began to advance beyond the infantile state of dependency (which was unquestionably forced upon them, and by no means of their own doing), they advanced and began to apply their gifts and talents for their own benefit, gain, and gratification. This thrust was short lived and often ended violently with the main casualties being the lives of American African people, their dreams, confidence and aspirations (Rosewood, Florida; "Black Wall Street" Tulsa, Oklahoma, etc.).

The resiliency is remarkable, for despite the horrendous experience dealt to American Africans, there has been a steady resurrection of their will and determination. It says alot about a group who can endure such catastrophic centuries, inch forward in utter confusion, and emerge semi-"successful"; it says even more about the oppressive and obstructive system that the American African, far and wide, has yet to learn to make a living for themselves. In agriculture, industry, and business, the modern American African still lacks sufficient power to be self-determining. In most cases, things have changed very little from when Dr. Woodson wrote:

> The Negroes of today are unable to employ one another, and the
> Whites are inclined to call on Negroes only when workers of their

own race have been taken care of. For the solution of this problem the "mis-educated" Negro has offered no remedy whatever. What Negroes are now being taught does not bring their minds into harmony with life as they must face it. (p. 38)

In today's ivory tower, we have HBCUs closing Africana Studies departments, in part due to the low enrollment of students. We have a situation where some students avoid that "Black stuff" at all costs. The closest thing to African socialization that many of today's students receive is the joining of a Historically Black Sorority or Fraternity...but even those are considered Greek. The mindset necessary for thinking productively and industriously about one's future and the gift of being able to take your family's assets, talents and bread-winning methodologies to the next level is all but vacant.

For example, how often do American Africans go to school with the intention of expanding upon their family business or to employ their parents, siblings and other kin folk at jobs they are already working for others? Somewhere, somehow, the idea of becoming self-sufficient has taken a negative turn. It is no longer a point of pride for numerous American African youth to be self-sufficient, to have a family business, or to have multiple generations self-sustaining in a particular trade, craft or industry, except of course if one can boast of having their own record label, production studio, or block from which to hustle.

It's highly similar to the "brain drain" experienced by both Caribbean and African nations once England and other European nations opened their borders to their ex-colonies. The "best and the brightest," (really just the most mobile) citizens left and/or sent their children to their "salvation and glory." Providing the opportunity to mix and mingle with those of the colonizer, never again to suffer the "lowly life" afforded them by their struggling nation. Again, the pursuit of opportunity is not a negative thing; it's when those children and upwardly mobile families leave and never look back, or when those families truly believe that their "lowly state" is because of their innate deficiencies, or when they truly believe that the "grand opportunities" provided by "the mother country" is because of the superiority of the former colonizers, that a problem exists. While there are many who go and send money and other material goods back "home," their newly developed skills, gifts, talents and psychological devotion are oft times relegated to the servicing of their new place of residence.

The author remembers traveling to a small West African nation wherein he lived for a short-time in a village. One day a conversation began about family structure and lifestyle. The author was asked where his mother lived in reference to his [the author's] own personal residence. The author was met with shock and disbelief when he stated his mother lived in another state, over two-hundred miles north. The village mentality could not fathom the benefit of taking an able-bodied man away from his birth-family indefinitely. It was explained that many from their village leave to develop skills and training, but they almost always return in order to continue building their home. In this rat race of a philosophy guiding the American dream, the American African is duped into chasing opportunities that he does not find, while forsaking those at-hand; oft-times neglecting those who cared most for them.

Part of the issue derives from the indiscriminate imitation of what the American African's have been given as examples of success. It is a natural human tendency to seek out successful examples of what they themselves are intending to do; however, it becomes tricky when there lacks a thorough evaluation of all variables contributing to the observed examples of success. In the case of the American African, the most readily available examples of success are their White counterparts. When an American African attempts to imitate the patterns of behavior that led to the observed success, they tend to come up short due to a lack of the same level of opportunity afforded the White example. Additionally, a significant portion of the content received during academic "training" is at best irrelevant for making a living, and at worst designed to intentionally produce incompetence, that is if there was any schooling at all.

The faithful arrogance associated with the strictly intellectual development of us and our progeny is our demise. The negative judgment directed towards those who manually labor and who have limited academic schooling is disgusting and a sad case of the blind attempting to lead the blind. For it seems to be the case that those who are independently productive and are able to express their creativity freely and according to their means are much more satisfied than those who are constantly trying to manipulate their situations in order to one day become "successful." The person who is skilled at using cloth diapers, planting food, carpentry, auto mechanics, etc. has peace of mind when it comes to consumer woes. The same person is often called upon by those who have "advance" degrees for assistance.

There was a time when the author needed a hot water heater replaced after the crawl-space under his house was flooded. While visiting the local hardware store assessing whether or not he could change it himself, he met an older gentleman who called himself a plumber. The plumber was actually loading up a water heater to install for someone else. The author immediately saw this as a sign and engaged the plumber, who was more than willing to assist and teach along the way. It wasn't until the third encounter that the former disclosed he had a Ph.D. in clinical psychology. This opened up an entirely different level of conversation regarding the lack of humility often encountered by the plumber when dealing with the "educated." He was totally surprised at the author's willingness and desire to learn about the "grunge-work" associated with manual labor; he was even more surprised by the author's humility and willingness to actually do it.

If there is to be any solution to the wide array of disparities and ills faced by American Africans, there must be a shift in this perspective regarding the ability to make a living. This shift must be in the direction of once again reclaiming the holistic, dual hemispheric, synthesis-driven perspective that once assisted in the construction of great African civilizations. This is not an attempt at romanticizing the past; but instead, is a clear point of observation, demonstrating the superior way of life maintained by Africans prior to the death blow dealt by enslavement and colonization, the proverbial "one-two punch."

No argument could successfully challenge the notion that Africans, globally, were negatively impacted by the invasion, enslavement and colonization of people, culture, resources and land by Europeans and Arabs. There is equally no argument to successfully challenge the notion that the more than 400 years of forced labor and enslavement created a psychological state of dependency and a general aversion to the behaviors that would support self-sufficiency (i.e., building shelter, growing food, bartering and trading within one's own community, educating one's own children).

The solution must address the false notion that industry and intellectualism are conflicting opposites. It must address the dependent psychological state of the American African, which is evidenced by the mass consumerism, as compared to the levels of productivity maintained by the population. There must also be provisions made to increase one's ability to see value in delaying gratification in order to also increase the likelihood that an individual will plan and implement strategies to obtain long-term goals. Additionally, learning to make a living must also entail the cultivation of an empowering perspective of one's self, culture, ancestry, capabilities and position in the world.

Since Dr. Woodson's time, there have been amazing strides and achievements by American Africans (some of which are undocumented or falsely attributed to another), thus there are plenty of models for designing a strategy based on the aforementioned criteria. There are literally cases where an enslaved African, upon emancipation, became a successful business person, property owner, self-sufficient and motivated contributor to their community, or a formal educator. Within a few generations, the American African community was able to boast of several institutions of higher education, thriving epicenters such as "Black Wall Street" in Tulsa, and respectable contributions to the artistic culture of the nation. Unfortunately, there has never been a critical mass of progressive American Africans to bring this scale to the tipping point, which would, theoretically, establish a system in which advancement would be a more permanent and common course for the masses of American Africans.

As stated by Woodson, it is necessary for American Africans to push beyond the crippling effects of a defeatist and dependent mentality; it is time to do the so-called impossible.

The "uneducated" Negro business man, however, is actually at work doing the very thing which the "mis-educated" Negro has been taught to believe cannot be done. This much-handicapped Negro business man could do better if he had some assistance, but our schools are turning out men who do as much to impede the progress of the Negro in business as they do to help him. *The trouble is that they do not think for themselves.* (emphasis added) If the "highly educated" Negro would forget most of the untried theories taught him in school, if he could see through the propaganda which has been instilled into his mind under the pretext of education, if he

would fall in love with his own people and begin to sacrifice for
their uplift—if the "highly educated" Negro would do these things,
he could solve some of the problems now confronting the race.
(p. 44)

A major key to bringing balance to this situation is to
incorporate valuable practical experience, in real world,
culturally relevant situations. For example, the author while
in pursuit of his doctoral degree in clinical psychology was
required to engage in at least 10 semesters of practical work
in the field of psychology, mental health, and social services.
There came a time where a decision had to be made regarding
the organization/agency through which the author would gain
these experiences. The options seemed infinite, each having
its strengths and weaknesses. When it came down to making
a final decision, only one agency possessed what it would
take for the author to become an expert at identifying and
alleviating the problems of American Africans from a culturally
specific and culturally relevant perspective.

It was extremely important that the orientation and
theoretical foundations of the organization match that of
the author's worldview as well as maintain a high level of
congruency with the people being serviced. There were
both subtle and not so subtle attempts to discourage the
author from going this route, including threats of pending
professional doom. Alternatives were offered, which also
dealt with American African populations, but from a European
worldview, which to the author, was not a real option. It is not
the author's belief that the guidance received around these
matters was given for malicious purposes, nor that those
providing the options were consciously attempting to thwart
the author's desires to assist his community. On the contrary,
the author believes that each of these individuals had the
author's best interest at heart, and was genuinely attempting to
assist the author in fulfilling his life's goals.

The above illustration is presented to demonstrate what Woodson says about students at our "Negro" schools (i.e., HBCUs). He notes that our students are not encouraged to do things to improve their communities and race, from a stance that is relevant to that community and/or race. Instead, they are taught to go along with the program, get a degree, and expect positions of leadership to be granted based on some illusory obligation:

> The schools in which Negroes are now being trained, however, do not give our young people this point of view. They may occasionally learn the elements...but they do not learn how to apply what they have studied. The training which they undergo gives a false conception of life when they believe that the business world owes them a position of leadership...Graduates of our business schools lack the courage to throw themselves upon their resources and work for a commission... They do not seem to realize that the great strides in business have been made by paying men according to what they do. (p. 46)

If nothing else is taken from this chapter, the reader should gain an understanding of what it truly means to make a living and to see how one may resist the directive to become comfortable in dependency. Seek strategies for balancing the intellectual with the practical, the theoretical with the proven, and the philosophical with the applicable. Do something everyday that requires you to use your hands (get some dirt under your nails!); also, read at least 30 minutes everyday about something that you do not know and that is relevant and beneficial in some way. Get into the habit of making yourself work hard to gain privilege and favor. Build a sense of confidence in your ability to grow and do better, and expect it to be so. Maintain a disposition of humility and receptivity in order that opportunities to learn may become identifiable to you. And perhaps most importantly, stay connected to your community and those with whom you seek mutual support; resist the flow of the "brain drain." Do not become one of the educated that *leaves the masses...*

Chapter Six

Lost Ones...
(The Educated Negro Leaves the Masses)

"Religion is but religion, if the people live up to the faith they profess."
Dr. Carter G. Woodson
The Mis-education of the Negro

"It's funny how money change a situation, miscommunication leads to confrontation."
Lauryn Hill
Lost Ones, The Mis-education of Lauryn Hill

"You're running and you're running and you're running away...but you can't run away from yourself!"
Bob Marley
Running Away

It is a very interesting observation that a great number of HBCUs are within a stone's throw of an impoverished American African community. It almost seems to taunt those in the community like a dog whose leash is just millimeters short of reaching its food bowl. Some have called this observation a mere coincidence. The author agrees that these are, in fact, co-incidents (coinciding events), not to be mistaken for the erroneous mis-definition of the word to mean "a random, and unrelated occurrence." The fall-out from such proximity is readily evidenced by the following: At an HBCU located in a large city "up-South," there is not a week that passes without a campus alert being issued regarding an assault and/or a robbery of one of its students by what is presumed to be a local citizen. At another HBCU, this one located in the mid-South, there is an unspoken rule that the admissions office not recruit from the surrounding high schools for fear that "the local element" would taint the "illustrious fabric" of the student body. The students constantly receive warnings in the form of cautionary statements to "never venture off campus, alone after dark" or "ladies, don't hook up with the local guys…they are all trouble."

With this type of interaction between our institutions of higher education and the surrounding communities, the fear of the latter and pure contempt for the former makes it all but impossible for a merger and healthy interaction between the two. Thus, many of our "highly-educated" American Africans matriculate for years, never once embracing the community surrounding their institutions; while the alienated neighborhood, in their contempt, no longer support the institutions and some even wish for its demise. Simultaneously, the children of the surrounding community that have dreams of attending college, paint a picture that does not include those HBCUs in their own backyard.

This scenario creates a situation where the local talent is whisked away to a "foreign" land to develop their skills and competencies, with most never to return to their hometown to contribute to the communities and institutions that surrounded them during their childhood. How would the American African community be different if the local institutions of higher education valued the surrounding community and pledged to uplift its development by recruiting from amongst their best and brightest, while simultaneously providing resources and programs for the adults? How much more advanced would Georgia Avenue in Washington, DC, Jefferson Street in Nashville, TN, or Greenwood Ave. in Baltimore be if Howard University, Tennessee State University, Fisk University, Meharry Medical College, and Morgan State University followed this proposal? It seems they would become grassroot stakeholders in these urban epicenters and would thusly develop a level of mutual respect, protecting the institutions, its students, and the community as a whole.

Oh, if only to dream…Now this section is not to dismiss or in any way negate the tremendous amounts of resources poured into the surrounding communities by the aforementioned HBCUs. In fact, much work has been done over the years and is currently underway (i.e., Fisk Univeristy's participation in J.U.M.P. [Jefferson Street United Merchants Partnership], Morgan State University's Community MILE initiative, etc.). Nonetheless, it seems that they can't quite get beyond the struggle and into fully flourishing and striving existences.

This modern day occurrence was prophesized by Dr. Woodson in the following statement:

> In our time too many Negroes go to school to memorize certain facts to pass examinations for jobs. After they obtain these positions they pay little attention to humanity…The "highly educated" Negroes have turned away from the people…and the gap between the masses and the "talented tenth" is rapidly widening. (p. 53)

Although speaking specifically of the American African church population, the above quote is easily and readily applicable to the HBCU. In fact, many American African churches direct much of their marketing efforts toward the student body of local colleges and universities. These students are seen as a hot commodity and a viable consumer of the services offered by the church. Local pastors and ministers provide internships and mentorships to students in religious studies programs, who are also offered courses on the "mega-church" and given opportunities to become shepherds of women and men.

A separatist mentality, when combined with intellectual prowess and spiritual/religious authority over a "flock" is a potentially dangerous mixture. This is due in large part to the lack of connectivity to the "souls" to be "saved" and to the "mega-church aspirations" (i.e., the desire to pastor a mega church) maintained by a large number of ministers, pastors and "religious studies" students alike. The masses tend to not be as "educated" and nowhere near as academically indoctrinated into the ways of church leadership, church culture, bible & religious history, and thus, they usually don't stand a chance in this arena; a situation eerily reminiscent of worship under plantation rule.

Dr. Woodson wrote:

> In the church, however, the Negro has had sufficient freedom to develop this institution in his own way; but he has failed to do so. His religion is merely a loan from the Whites who have enslaved and segregated the Negroes; and the organization, though largely an independent Negro institution, is dominated by the thought of the oppressors of the race. The "educated" Negro minister is so trained as to drift away from the masses and the illiterate preachers into whose hands the people inevitably fall are unable to develop a doctrine and procedure of their own. The dominant thought is to make use of the dogma of the Whites as means to an end. Whether the system is what it should be or not it serves the purpose.
>
> (p. 57-58)

To use the dogma of the oppressor during enslavement and immediately upon its termination is understandable, however, in 2012 it seems to be counterproductive and perhaps a self-inflicted and fatal wound. For example, in today's church, there still remains a Caucasian image of Jesus the Christ. Clinical psychiatrist Dr. Frances Cress Welsing deals deeply with the implications of such an image being held so dear and so highly in the American African psyche. She notes that to give "the only begotten Son of God" features of a European, is to also make God a European. She continues by explaining how identifying a man with European features as the Savior for all of humanity (the majority of which are non-White and were historically enslaved or colonized by Europeans) does deep psychological damage by establishing a dependency on the oppressor for one's concept of freedom and salvation.

Some of the more "progressive" institutions have acknowledged and sought to address this issue by totally removing all images of God and Jesus from within their place of worship. The typical overt explanation for such an action is usually related to the scripture that no graven images shall be formed or the notion that "His color does not matter." But what of the institution that decides to take it a step further and, without apology, follows the description of Jesus the Christ as written in the Holy Bible by offering a non-White image?

The first chapter of Revelations gives a symbolic description including feet of brass, which appear to have been placed in fire based on their glow, and wooly hair. While all serious biblical scholars would have to agree that Jesus could not have possessed the features consistent with the popular Europeanized depictions maintained deep within the mind's of Christians and non-Christians alike, there seems to be a need to argue against anyone who attempts to challenge this false notion. Part of the oppressive nature of the church is that it does not dare break free from the traditions carried over from the days when the first American African preachers in the "New World" were force fed the enslaver's notions of Christianity and ordained to control the rest of the plantation. Today it looks a little different, but still maintains the same level of confusion, docility and passivity among its congregations.

By no means is this an attack on the church, Christianity, or Christians. This is merely an observation of but a portion of the aforementioned aspects of the faith. In fact, the church remains one of the most stable and powerful institutions in the American African community, despite its vast divisions and various denominations. To ascribe to a specific denomination helps a person to fine-tune their brand of worship, faith, and belief. This is not the problem; the problem is created when people of differing denominations of the same religion begin to accuse the others of being incorrect and false representations of the faith. In one example, Woodson wrote of a community wherein there were approximately ten families. These families all ascribed to their own denominations and were thus unable to form a church amongst themselves. Woodson maintains that this division across denomination is an imitation and direct result of the quarrels within the European church.

In addition to the division by denomination, the business model of the modern church makes it almost necessary for church leaders to increase their recruitment efforts through the use of marketing tools (i.e., radio & television commercials, billboards, newspaper ads, word of mouth, etc.) and further distinguish their message from that of others. The author has attended several American African churches and at times felt he was at a Wu Tang Clan concert based on the number of people on stage with the minister delivering the word. The number of church employees is a touchy topic for obvious reasons, the most apparent being the fact that people are being employed. In some churches, the pastor has a representative, who has a representative, who also has an assistant representative, making it almost impossible to reach the pastor. As in Woodson's day, there is a large duplication of roles and services in the church and HBCU alike; in the case of the latter you have vice presidents in large and perhaps unnecessary numbers.

Some churches have building funds and projects in the millions of dollars and lean heavily on their congregations to contribute. This pressure is enough to turn away those who are able to think beyond the feelings of guilt delivered from the pulpit. The author remembers attending a church some years ago, in support of a close friend who had answered the call to minister. After one of their sermons, the pastor began to prepare the congregation for tithing. He called for everyone sitting at the end of the pew closest to the center aisle to become the "pew leader." This leader was to then count the number of persons in their row. Once the number was obtained, each row was to pass their tithing envelopes to the leader, who was to make sure they had one for each person in the pew.

As the crowd settled down after following the instructions, the pastor asked if anyone had a discrepancy. One lady raised her hand. The pastor asked how many she was short, she replied "One." The pastor then changed his tone as if to reflect anger and asked, "Who in that row did not tithe!?!" A little girl of about 8 years of age timidly raised her hand. He yelled at her, "Where is your mother?," to which the little girl replied with a gesture as a woman in the pew behind her slowly raised her hand. The pastor then continued to chastise the parent with such threats as: "How dare you keep your daughter from receiving the blessings of God because you refused to give her money to make her tithes," and "You would really keep your daughter from going to heaven just because you were too cheap to give her something for the offering plate?" He concluded, "If you want her to get her blessings, you better give her some money and an envelope to put in that plate!" The woman was embarrassed, but complied without hesitation…Needless to say, the author never visited that church again.

One of Dr. Woodson's most poignant points in this chapter has to do with the "theology of foreigners." He identifies how the main theses utilized by ministers in the American African church are based upon notions championed by what he calls "pagans." He highlights the fact that much of the hardships and otherwise heinous assaults on humanity were actually sanctioned by theologians, who seem to have taken up the banner of deception, manipulation, whoremongering, sexual & physical assault, enslavement, and most things unholy. Aside from the occasional scandal involving a minister, bishop, or pastor of an American African church, it seems that the modern church, while connected with the larger body, maintains some basic tenants that keep it separate from the larger, European controlled church body. Nonetheless, choosing to follow blindly has its consequences; the confusion and passivity, or the sheer lack of initiative to mobilize and concentrate the financial and resource capital of the American African community stands as a shining example.

The indiscriminate imitation and perpetuation of this brand of Christianity, as developed, taught and maintained by racist White men is perhaps one of the greatest flaws of the American African church. There is very little practical religious and spiritual science taught or even discussed in the church. The missing 18 years of Jesus' life is rarely, if ever, touched upon. The immaculate conception of his cousin John the Baptist, the mistaking of John for Jesus based on his actions, the amazing miracles and statements affirming the ability of others to do the same are all excellent starting points for the empowerment of American African congregations. To discuss all of the ways of Egypt that Moses was learned in and how this influenced both Judaism and Christianity would serve to prove more beneficial than the ability to shout and sing and give the outward appearance of praise.

Another major area for improvement in the American African church is that of physical health as it relates to diet. One can readily find in the Old Testament dietary guidelines for those who profess to be spiritual leaders, priests and ministers. There was clear objection to the consumption of pig flesh by Jesus and his forefathers; in fact, the Levites, aside from the occasional consumption of the sacrificial meats, were vegetarian. The shift to a health conscious message by the American African church would revolutionize the staggering health disparities suffered by its membership. Additionally, if the church became a financial institution with the purpose of developing the well-being of its community and its member's economic status by way of education, investment opportunities, job placement, drug rehab, psychological and social services, the condition of the American African community would undergo a drastic and expedient change.

Why then are these things not addressed by the church leaders as a principle upon which all churches stand? It's the author's opinion that it is directly related to what Woodson called "degenerate learning" which serves as "the avenue of the oppressor's propaganda." (p. 61) If one would simply begin to think and decide for one's self, as many have done, the churches will either be empty or forced to enhance their programs to address the real needs as presented by a critical and conscious mass of the community which it proposes to serve. Unfortunately, by ascribing to "blind faith" and unquestioning devotion, many followers of American African church leaders have relinquished their power for self-determination, and accept the yoke of servitude without real reward. In Woodson's words, the American African church:

> …has prevented the union of diverse elements and has kept
> the race too weak to overcome foes who have purposely taught
> Negroes how to quarrel and fight about trifles until their enemies
> can overcome them. This is the keynote to the control of the so-

called inferior races by the self-styled superior. The one thinks and plans while the other in excited fashion seizes upon and destroys his brother with whom he should cooperate. (p. 61)

Those who have been educated beyond their ability to be coerced into following this path of destruction have removed themselves from amongst the number, and have sought their own methods of worshipping their concept of divinity. The bad in this is the fact that it further divides the "highly" or "mis-educated" from the so-called "uneducated" masses. There seems to be no common ground where the two can meet within the church to discuss the need for refinement of the message to meet the true needs of the people.

Without this connection, many are left to fend for themselves in an arena, as previously pointed out, in which they don't stand a chance. The rewarding of rhetoric and the mastery and memorization of information coupled with the ability to argue, has taken the place of critical, synthetical and analytical thinking skills; thus allowing for the dominance of ignorant fools with good memories over those who can reason, question and understand that things aren't quite right. Leaving the once rebellion-prone rabble-rouser to acquiesce in silence while internally suffering, and thus, creating a class of weak-willed, cowardice traitors of the race. Hence Dr. Woodson's next chapter: *Dissension and Weakness*.

Chapter 7

Only As Strong As the Weakest Link
(Dissension and Weakness)

"Supreme excellence consists in breaking the enemy's resistance without fighting."
Sun Tzu, The Art of War

"To divide and rule is their whole plan…"
Sizzla and Jah Cure
Kings in this Jungle

The ease with which American African individuals, groups, and institutions are led to talk negatively about one another, or even worse, plan actions to insult, injure or neutralize their "competition" is a sure sign of sickness. It's akin to an autoimmune disease, wherein the body is not recognized by the defense systems, and thus is attacked as if it were the enemy. A consistent and strong enough attack on the body eventually begins to wear the body down to the point where it is unable to protect itself from any outside force, leaving it totally vulnerable to any and all invaders.

Now, more so than in Woodson's time, there is a dire need for the ability to discern the subtleties that distinguish friend from foe. This is so, because of the way that racism and racists undergo a complex system of refinement. For example, in the

1930s, American African's were being hanged from trees and hunted down by lynch mobs, castrated and even burned alive. Today, the lynching is much more sophisticated and the mob is not as easy to recognize. Many of today's potential victims of race-based "lynching" fail to realize the major purpose of lynching, which is to intimidate and neuter (neutralize), and thus fail to comprehend the many methods by which American Africans continue to be rendered fearfully impotent.

To create dissension amongst a group is a sure way to weaken its abilities to function in its own best interest. So for all of the Civil Rights, Human Rights, and justice seeking organizations that exist for the benefit of the American African, many are incapable of uniting and organizing with another group. A prime example of this inability is seen annually during Kwanzaa week, when in various cities around the nation African-centered organizations plan multiple events and activities at competing and conflicting times; or how our numerous independent, American African and African-centered schools are unwilling and/or unable to unite and form an American African/African-centered school "system" (a notion that differs from the excellent work of CIBI – Council of Independent Black Institutions). It is even evidenced by the situation where HBCUs neighboring each other, stand by and watch as their neighbors are slowly being disassembled for financial and accreditation issues; never once entertaining the option of merging and forming a stronger force to be reckoned with.

We can echo these same sentiments when it comes to spiritual and religious institutions. Like liquor stores and barbershops, you can find a plethora of churches, mosques, synagogues, temples, lodges, and various "houses of worship" lining block after block in some of the most impoverished, and predominately American African communities. These various institutions rarely bring about any formidable change in the overall safety, health, and appearance of the surrounding community, but instead, often leech resources from the already strapped citizens.

In some of the more progressive cities, there is also a healthy number of more "traditional" organizations. Traditional in this context refers to those forms of worship that are closely related to the indigenous practices of pre-enslavement Africans, including their spiritual and ritual sciences. Except among the latter groups, will one consistently find inter-faith participation in the upliftment and universal concern for the community-at-large. Having participated in both "mainstream" and "traditional" ceremonies, rituals and organizing events, the author finds this statement to be true, more times than not. One example is a group functioning out of Washington, DC that gathers all of the local "houses" of traditional African-centered spiritual and educational organizations. One such gathering occurred as the author happened to be passing through town to meet with a spiritual teacher. An invitation to participate in an upcoming ceremony was extended and accepted. The author took it as a blessing and immediately rearranged his schedule to accommodate the event.

The ceremony was a call to action; it was to take place in Richmond, Virginia and concerned a recently discovered enslaved African burial ground, now covered by a corporate parking lot. The various organizations met at the site and performed one mass ceremony; each having the opportunity to perform their sacred rites and other pre-assigned duties. It was beautiful. The unity of Vodoun, Ifa, Akan, Kemetic, and various other communities with their respective languages of praise and worship, dances, clothing, and subtle nuances was perhaps one of the most brilliant experiences in this author's young life. The mutual respect, reverence, honor and love demonstrated is impossible to fake. The power behind this gathering was evidenced by an inner calm and knowing, even amongst "strangers" from as far away as Florida.

This does not mean that there is no dissension within these groups of "traditional" religious institutions. On the contrary, there have been just as many scandals and accusations of corruption to visit these orders, as the Catholic or Baptist Church. For example, one leader was recently charged, in a public on-line forum of having physically and sexually abused women and under-aged girls, while another has been incarcerated for the trafficking of children. There also exist countless stories of practitioners seeking to use their "spiritual powers" to bring harm to someone of their same or another orientation.

If only these religious groups and organizations would set aside their differences and unite. A shining example of the ability and willingness to unite across faith was the First African Baptist Church on Sapelo Island. The then recently emancipated Africans formed a congregation that met in a Christian church and maintained a hybrid style of worship that combined both Islamic and Christian beliefs and practices. One of the most noted was the strong belief in facing East during prayer, as well as burying the body with the footstone to the East so on "Judgment Day," when the body is risen it will already be facing the East.

If somehow the estimated 200 million + Christians living in the United States could come together with the estimated 1 to 5 million Muslims living in this nation, for the common purpose of ensuring peace, order, justice and the healthy growth and development of all children, the nation would find itself in a far more socially advanced state. Instead, what we find is dissension within these groups, oft times divided along the denomination line. Separate factions of the same religion quarrel in an attempt to prove the authenticity of their own views, while simultaneously attempting to invalidate that of the other. The saddest part is that all lose in the end, with the children suffering the most. It pretty much dooms the future to carry on the "beef" of the preceding generation, relegating them to a lesser existence, void of the insight necessary to reroute and sublimate the battle-locked energy, into more productive and constructive avenues. This my friends, is a true "generational curse."

To speak of and identify weaknesses is something that can be over-emphasized in today's deficit-based society. Nonetheless, it is a necessary commentary if one is to seek a true solution to the issues facing the citizens of this planet. Unfortunately, many fail to understand the real issues to be addressed; and for those who do understand the real issues, the depth of impact is yet to be discovered. The notion of "mis-education" is synonymous with the rendering of ignorance. Ignorance is found to be at the root of most fear (False Evidence Appearing Real) and violence, two things that are as American as apple pie. It is an amazing fact that with all of our highly educated American African religious leaders, the science necessary for true behavior modification in the form of spiritual evolution continues to elude so many.

Isn't it interesting that when a person goes to dental school they emerge as a dentist, yet many individuals that enroll in divinity school experience nothing of a divine transformation, nor the instruction to lead one in the direction towards emerging divine? Again, the demonstration of true worthiness has been replaced with the ability to remember and regurgitate, pass intellectual examinations, and appear according to the expectations of the gatekeepers (a sad fact that is applicable across disciplines and is evidenced by the Cancer Center employee that smokes cigarettes, the mechanic with a broken down vehicle, or the barber with a poor fade). Is this why an individual can become an internationally known religious leader while simultaneously raping children? Or how religious leaders can intentionally inspire fear and terror in populations for the sole purpose of maintaining control and generating profits? Whatever happened to character development?

A man once shared with the author that he is confused and distressed by his wife's enjoyment the of music by a popular artist who had been charged with the sexual abuse of a minor. The wife, who considered herself to be a devoted Christian, rationalized and explained her support of the artist by "separating his talents from his actions." This position troubled her spouse who felt that the separation of actions from a person's character based on their ability to hold a note was virtually impossible. "He is his actions," exclaimed the husband.

Reconciliation of the contradiction was impossible in the husband's mind, who no longer trusted the authenticity of his wife's professed devotion. This story is shared only because it brings up a very powerful and oft times under addressed issue that floats around the American African community: the notion of morality not being a prerequisite of religious leadership and social role modeling. It strangely approaches the supposed sanctity of the priest who governed plantation prisoners, while simultaneously raping and physically assaulting their congregation.

Almost anybody of the lowest type may get into the Negro ministry... As evidence of the depths to which the institution has gone a resident of Cincinnati recently reported a case of its exploitation by a railroad man who lost his job and later all his earnings in a game in a den of vice in that city. To refinance himself he took an old black frock coat and a Bible and went into the heart of Tennessee, where he conducted at various points a series of distracted, protracted meetings which netted him two hundred and ninety-nine converts to the faith and four hundred dollars in cash...The large majority of Negro preachers of today, then, are doing nothing more than to keep up the mediaeval hell-fire scare which the Whites have long since abandoned... (pp. 68-69)

Is there truly a profit associated with the maintenance of ignorance, fear, and violence? If Christians were truly developed to become Christ-like, and if Muslims were taught the practical applications of the Pillars of Islam what industries would suffer as a result? If the various religious institutions became what they proclaim, who would stand to suffer? The answers to the above questions would surely lead to the root of the problem. For example, how would the prison industry, trauma centers, infectious disease treatment facilities, drug and alcohol related rehabilitation centers/treatment programs, and many aspects of media fare if the masses decided to follow their religious and spiritual tenants without apology. This author's guess is that they would crumble without hesitation.

It is as if the mis-education of the masses is for the sole purpose of keeping them hopeless in the face of change. Almost as if mis-education is designed to produce weakness, which in turn, leaves one vulnerable to dissension. In the church, this mis-education creates confusion around the notions of holiness and righteousness.

Recently an observer saw a result of this in the sermon of a Negro college graduate, trying to preach to a church of the masses. He referred to all the great men in history of a certain country to show how religious they were, whether they were or not. When he undertook to establish the Christian character of Napoleon, however, several felt like leaving the place in disgust...Here, then, was a case of the religion of the pagan handed down by the enslaver and segregationist to the Negro. (p. 65)

A modern manifestation of the above quote was demonstrated when a well known Christian minister exclaimed with great conviction that Haiti, who had recently experienced a massive earthquake, was cursed by God for adhering to their traditional spiritual and religious practices. He stated that the inhabitants of this resource-rich island had participated in wicked acts, which had offended God, and thus were rewarded with great destruction. There were many Haitians who shared sentiments with this minister; some even led "witch-hunts" to assist in cleansing Haiti of her "devilish" inhabitants.

Through all of this, never did this author hear any mention in mainstream media of the wicked acts visited upon the people of Haiti by the French and Spanish who served as their Lord and Master for centuries as colonizers and enslavers. Never once did this author hear of a correlation being drawn between the impoverished state of Haiti and the post emancipation embargoes and military assaults waged by the West. There were American Africans who joined the "pro-Christian, anti-other" bandwagon, asking God to forgive the transgressions of Haiti, but never once calling into question the morality of the one with the megaphone declaring God's dissatisfaction. By the way, it was the same Napoleon mentioned in the above quote that was responsible for much of Haiti's historical hardship.

Oft times traditional forms of worshiping God are described as superstitious or fetish-based pseudo-religions. This same description is also used to discuss the religious and spiritual practices ascribed to by many of our more rural and "uneducated" American Africans living in the southern regions of the United States. These individuals, who tend to carry over the amalgamated religions handed down from pre-enslavement African to enslaved African to emancipated American African, continue to utilize various roots, herbs, symbols, "washes" and prayers, to address day-to-day circumstances.

The "good reverend doctors," with all of their education, oft times are incapable of respecting the origins and effectiveness of such practices because it was not a major part of their academic training; instead, it is relegated to a course, or segment of a course, entitled "Folk Religions" in which the philosophy and spiritual "materia medica" of these groups are ridiculed and minimized.

The examination of this ridicule leads to what is, perhaps, the most important question to be asked: What is the role of religious institutions in the mis-education, hence, the continued oppression of American Africans? Is it possible for ministers, who were taught by ministers, who were taught by ministers, who were taught by slave masters, to really establish and maintain a church based on liberation theology? If so, is unity with other religious-based institutions also a possibility? The field of ministry is becoming a rapidly growing interest of college students. More and more students are beginning to see this profession as a viable and lucrative option. Interestingly, there is a simultaneous decline in the number of students who value the development of practical skills, and have become increasingly "dumbed down" in regards to their abilities to demonstrate any semblance of self-sufficiency. This combination has the potential to thrust the American African deeper into the cycle of dependency, lack of self-determination, and spiritual stagnation.

This was the great argument between W.E.B. Du Bois and Booker T. Washington. If only they could have agreed to understand how both positions work to serve the upliftment of the recently emancipated Africans. One could only imagine the outcome of a system of education geared towards making one both intellectually savvy and practically skilled within the same process and curriculum; instead, we have generations believing that being a "cool fool" is more important than being practically intelligent and professional. Is this the natural disposition of the American African? Hardly. On the contrary, this situation is a direct result of the systematic discouraging of professional development as expounded upon in Dr. Woodson's next chapter, "*Professional Education Discouraged.*"

Chapter 8

Teach One To Fish
(Professional Education Discouraged)

"The people inna deh West the whole of dem ah go crazy. Love fi big up dem chest yet dem no end no slavery. They cyaan, yum no food without no money, so foolish is the man in fruitful Zion yet him hungry!"

Sizzla
One Way

A recent article published in a periodical for higher education identified what is considered to be a problem. The highlighted issue is that only 1% of all Ph.D.s in physics are earned by American Africans, a population they consider to be an ignored "intellectual resource." This is fascinating in that across all fields of science, technology, engineering and mathematics (STEM), there is pretty much the same report. As in Woodson's day, American Africans in the 21st century are still finding it difficult to gain access to and successfully matriculate through the process of becoming a trained and licensed professional in many trades. This is the same for licensed psychologists, certified teachers, lawyers, medical doctors, dentists, contractors, brick masons, social workers, plumbers, electricians, HVAC techs, etc. in many states.

This is not unique to the U.S., but is a global phenomenon in all but the predominately non-White nations on the planet. For example, the UK boasts of a mere 50 "Black" professors of the 140,000 (.003%) throughout their universities. This fact supports Woodson's notion that:

> Most Whites in contact with Negroes, always the teachers of their brethren in black, both by precept and practice, have treated the professions as aristocratic spheres to which the Negroes should not aspire. We have had, then, a much smaller number than those who under different circumstances would have dared to cross the line; and those that did so were starved out by the Whites who would not treat them as a professional class...Negroes, then, learned from their oppressors to say to their children that there were certain spheres into which they should not go because they would have no chance therein for development...Few had the courage to face the ordeal; and some professional schools and institutions for Negroes were closed about thirty to forty years ago, partly on this account...This was especially true of the law schools, closed during the wave of legislation against the Negro, at the very time the largest possible number of Negroes needed to know the law for the protection of their civil and political rights. In other words, the thing which the patient needed most to pass the crisis was taken from him that he might more easily die. (p. 76)

Many fail to recognize that such practices were and still are in place, and that the purposeful dumbing down of American Africans is a systematic and oft times subtle occurrence. An analogy the author developed some years ago while serving the Ministry of Education in St. Kitts and Nevis will help to illustrate this confusion well:

> *If a row of dominoes could talk, and after they had been lined up and knocked down were asked, "Who knocked you over?" If speaking to the 4th domino, it would surely reply either the 3rd or the 5th domino, depending on the direction of the fall. In reality, it was the individual that set the dominos up in such a manner that they would all fall into each other who is entirely responsible for the situation. Yet this is done in such a skillful way, that all are confused...leaving each domino to blame the one next to it.*

Just as the dominoes in the above illustration blame each other for the inevitable fall, many American Africans also blame their own incompetency, failure to support, and lack of confidence in their own, as the reason their institutions are often times substandard and have either failed or are barely surviving.

The author was once fortunate to listen to a presentation given by the former president of an HBCU in the mid-South who was currently the dean of a law school at another HBCU in the deep South. This gentleman told the story of how the HBCU's law school had been cut-off from their funding sources and "taken over" by a neighboring predominately White institution (PWI). This PWI literally came over to the HBCU's campus and took their law library (all of the books, although they left the building); for proof the presenter said you could still find certain books at the PWI's law library with the stamp of the HBCU's name within its pages.

The dean was not on a mission to agitate the undergraduate crowd he was addressing, but instead was on a mission to recruit for the redeveloping law school. He had declared some 13 years earlier that he would assist in the reclaiming of the law school and now was at the phase of enrolling the best and the brightest students nationwide from other HBCUs. His offer was hard to refuse; a student with a 3.5 grade point average (GPA) was eligible for a "full-ride" and guaranteed job placement to work as an apprentice which would assist the student to fulfill the requirements of the National Bar Association. Three years later, our paths crossed once again, this time in an elevator of yet another HBCU "up-South" where the dean was still on his mission to recruit the best and the brightest from HBCU undergraduate programs.

Having worked in public schools in both southern and

northern states, the author has had enough contact hours to speak authoritatively on the subject of high school guidance counselors and how they boldly discourage American African youth from pursuing college degrees. In the case where the student is persistent and sure about going to college, they are often steered towards PWIs and away from HBCUs, even if there are several in their hometown. In many conversations with freshmen college students and high school seniors, it is found that they were never made aware of the opportunity to attend an HBCU; their parents, many of which were not college graduates themselves, did not have the network nor the experience to expose their children to the institutions of higher education within their own communities.

One such conversation took place in Nashville, Tennessee, which is home to four HBCUs. The student was a native to Nashville and a freshman enrolled at one of these HBCUs, one student spoke of how they had to openly challenge their guidance counselor when it came to their desire to attend an HBCU. The most malignant part of the situation is that the high school was literally on the same street as the university and in fact, had been given its land by that very institution.

The student explained that as an honor student, the guidance counselor thought they would fare better at a PWI which "had the resources to stimulate and support" the developing mind of their students. Such a notion is in fact a passive assault on the integrity and ability of an HBCU to do the same; students faced with such a proposition are often incapable of clearly articulating their disagreement. For those who are marginal in their academic performance, their experience is much different, if not all together non-existent. They may be ushered into programs such as Job Corps, or given applications to minimum wage jobs in their local communities; few are lucky enough to receive an application to a local community college as a potential and viable next step. These things are not bad options in the author's perspective. It becomes a problem when these options are disproportionately offered to American Africans without consideration or in spite of their ability and desire to pursue other avenues of formal academic training.

It is the author's belief that college is not a necessary and best next step for all; however, professional skills training and development is of the utmost importance for anyone who wants to perform as a functioning adult in this society. The author also posits that it is not enough for children to simply go to college, but to choose those institutions that properly prepare them to think and function as a mature and capable individual in a society fueled by racism. This is not advocating for the adoption and propagation of the "victim's mentality" but for a course of empowerment for those who have become confused, hopeless and helpless under the pressures of ignorance and racism.

As noted by Woodson, many of the best and brightest American African minds are blindly sent to institutions and find themselves in a world of hurt and isolation. Many students at PWIs often lament at conferences and social activities about their depression and feelings of loneliness. Perhaps the most stressful of all their experiences comes down to one of two occurrences: 1) being the only American African in their class and the expectation to be the spokesperson for the race; and 2) being one of a few American Africans and trying to fit in with the majority White population by not acting "too Black" and by acting "White enough" to get along with their classmates.

Outside of the aforementioned contexts, there is another major influence that presents as a more formidable opponent to the professional desires of American African youth in the 21st century. It seems that the vast majority of American African youth have as their primary goal to enter upon the career path of becoming a professional rapper, music producer, deejay or athlete. There is nothing inherently wrong with any of these aspirations, it's the motivational tools that the author takes issue with. As a former deejay and one who has grown up with and now studies hip hop culture, the author has applied a significant amount of thought and research hours to understanding the role of hip hop music and popular culture on the professional desires of American African youth.

Unbeknownst to the masses, the manipulation of tastes and desires is a daily affair. Many of our dreams and aspirations come from what we are exposed to on a daily basis; those things that are portrayed in a "more attractive" manner, are viewed as desirable and those that are presented as "unattractive" are less desired. Hence in the realm of the American African, who is already at a low point in regards to income, employment, and education may often see their parents and family members struggling at low paying and oft times stressful jobs, while simultaneously observing athletes and hip hop artist flaunting million dollar contracts (real or contrived), fame, sex, and power while enjoying life to the fullest. It is no wonder why many children aspire to be like the latter group. Their day-to-day life is more of a punishment than a reward. They seek to improve upon their situation in a manner that has been "demonstrated" to bring success; the problem is that the demonstration is false. In the case where the demonstrated success is indeed real, in many instances, there are maladaptive and dangerous activities associated with that success (i.e., drug dealing, gangster and thuggish behaviors/attitudes), which makes it likely that the aspirant will be incarcerated before they actually fulfill their dream of becoming a successful entertainer.

It is likely that many more would and could be successful

at their attempts to become entertainers if they were more thoroughly trained and professionally prepared to thrive and excel to the upper crest of their chosen craft. So for the child who wants to become a rapper or hip hop artist, it would be great for them to receive professional training as a writer and eventually become a master of oration and word delivery. Acting is also closely related to the world of hip hop, not in the sense that rappers are now beginning to appear in movies, but in the sense that many are literally actors, portraying the life of a fictional character. This sort of approach to becoming a rapper not only serves to enhance the quality of the presentation, but also opens up wide the world of opportunities for those who take this path. For example, the aspiring rapper can also author books, write for magazines and other print media, can teach creative writing, deliver speeches and talks for a fee, etc. They can contribute to the positively creative aspects of the culture similar to the multi-talented artists of the Harlem Renaissance.

It is interesting how the natural gifts of children are no longer systematically honed and enhanced through practice, but instead, taken for granted and assumed to be fully developed. This attitude betrays a bit of laziness as well as a point of arrogance when it comes to the American African. The pride of arrogance is what rationalizes the lack of desire for further training; however, it is also the seed of insecurity that promotes the false bravado and confidence associated with such a position. Hence, the majority of wannabes end up stifled in an immature expression of what is potentially an example of masterful craftsmanship.

In this assertion is the idea that because the Negro is good at dancing, joking, minstrelsy and the like he is "in his place" when "cutting a shine" and does not need to be trained to function in the higher sphere...and instead of increasing the prestige of the Negro they have brought the race into disgrace (p. 79).

Woodson continues:

> We scarcely realize what a poor showing we make in dramatics in spite of our natural aptitude in this sphere. Only about a half dozen Negro actors have achieved greatness, but we have more actors and showmen than any other professionals except teachers and ministers. Where are these thousands of men and women in the histrionic sphere?...Most of these would-be artists have no preparation for the tasks undertaken. (p. 79-80)

This author has encountered much "push back" for maintaining the perspective outlined above, but holds firmly to these statements. There have been encounters with people who passionately declare "I am hip hop" and that they would "die for hip hop" because it is their "life's purpose." The passion maintained by these individuals is totally understandable, owing to the sense of accomplishment and value one gains by being good at the art of hip hop. Nonetheless, there is no denying that this close association with forms of entertainment is potentially crippling. It removes all objectivity needed to thoroughly analyze the impact and potential negative influence of such an entity.

As mentioned by Mr. Neely Fuller, Jr. "until you understand racism (White supremacy), what it is and how it functions, everything else you think you understand will only confuse you." It is clear that many of the hip hop generation fail to understand the larger picture and role of the "hip hop culture" in the continuation of a racist agenda. It is also apparent that the mode of expression known as hip hop is a very powerful tool and it is here to stay. As such, it is of the utmost importance for those of us who are willing and able, to begin to deconstruct and reconstruct this medium in order that it may be used as a method for healing, correct education and positive identity development.

Entertainment and labor are but two of the nine areas of people activity categorized by Mr. Fuller and reflected upon in this chapter, however, there is a third area that fits closely with these, politics. In his next chapter, Woodson delves into this area which deals specifically with people interactions, explaining how *Political Education Neglected*, enhances the detrimental nature of mis-education.

Dumbin' Down

Chapter 9

The Politics of Neglect
(Political Education Neglected)

*"Democracy. Crazy demo. Democracy. Demonstration of
craze. Democracy. Crazy demonstration."*

Fela Anikulapo Kuti
Teacher Don't Teach Me Nonsense

"We the people of the United States of America…"
These famous words are perhaps the most popular verbal relic
of this great nation. Written by men who saw fit to establish a
"more perfect union" of like-minded individuals, the pre-amble
of the U.S. Constitution is a very powerful and misunderstood
document. The vast levels of misunderstanding found amongst
the average U.S. citizen stem directly from a lack of exposure
to and study of this all-important document. Some would argue
that it is simply neglected and overlooked in the classroom,
while others believe it to be an instrumental part of the
dumbing down process.

The Constitution documents the highest laws of the land
and gives the ultimate ruling (executed by the Supreme Court)
on legal matters not handled on the State, County, or Local
levels of government. It is here that one can find their "rights"
as a citizen of the United States of America, and it is here that
one can catch a glimpse of the perspectives of the Founding
Fathers.

It is very interesting to note that simultaneous to and after the writing and signing of this document, there were Africans being branded, lynched, tortured, raped, captured, kidnapped, and held against their will without having committed a crime. In fact, there were specific clauses and articles giving the terms by which one could continue to kidnap and import Africans into the country (Article I, Section 9), while others (Article IV, Section 2) made it illegal to assist an enslaved African who had escaped, and even made it lawful to return the person to their state of captivity. The States with economies based on the enslavement of Africans and their forced labor on plantations were given a 20 year grace period by Article V, which forbade any amendments to challenge the rules for importing enslaved Africans to the U.S. until 1808.

This injustice would continue under the hoodwinked eyes of "Lady Justice" for an additional 178 years (from 1787 – 1965) under various forms, but with the same levels of criminality and cruelty. Many who have been wronged under this banner (the U.S. Constitution) have sought to oppose its validity by citing the hypocrisy of the authors who maintained the institution of Chattel Slavery while claiming, "all Men are created equal"; others have sought to use its power for their own benefit.

In line with W.E. Cross' model of "Nigrescence," this author feels that many African descendants here in the U.S. have at one time or another been on both ends of the scale. Typically, when one becomes aware of the injustices that have taken place against themselves, their communities or loved ones, they potentially become angered and seek to disassociate with any and everything that relates to the perpetrators of the injustice. They will attempt to totally withdraw into Blackness while avoiding and demonizing everything to do with Whiteness.

For example, a dear friend once stated that while going through this phase he literally painted his white toilet paper black to avoid the use of white tissue paper on his body. He jokes about it now, but during that time, he was highly emotional and attempting to heal from the direct and vicarious trauma he'd experienced while learning of his ancestor's hardships in this nation. This disposition usually leads the individual on a quest for more information that will empower their perspective of their own group as an oppressed population.

A person that is able to cope and adapt, slowly proceeds from this phase into the next where they begin to slowly reintegrate themselves into society, while maintaining their pro-African/pro-Black perspective; the difference is that the anti-White sentiments have been greatly relaxed. This phase tends to carry less emotional stress and allows for a clear approach to repairing the psychological damage and trans-generational trauma associated with enslavement, Jim Crowism, and racism (individual, systematic, group, etc.). This is the part in the chess game where the black pieces change their orientation from playing "defense-offense" to playing "offense-defense." This is key and pivotal because it allows one to go from a basic reactionary stance, to one of strategy and proactive movement.

The individual who continues to intentionally move forward, fully re-integrates into society accepting the best of themselves, their own culture and history, while simultaneously utilizing the best of other cultures around them, including that of the dominant and oppressive group. This individual tends to thrive on their own accord and pushes forward to learn to play the hand they have been dealt, and has an attitude and a desire to win. One such individual is Mr. Neely Fuller, Jr. He, like former Congressman Oscar De Priest (mentioned by Dr. Woodson), distributed copies of the U.S. Constitution to people who were interested in "replacing White supremacy (racism) with justice." In fact, the author received his first and only copy of the constitution in this manner. Mr. Fuller would express, against all ridicule and doubters, that the best way to establish justice amongst the people of the U.S. is for everyone to be equally aware of the laws that govern this land. He would place special emphasis on the 14th and 8th amendments, citing due process & equal protection and the prevention of cruel & unusual punishment, respectively.

These two very powerful amendments are useful when understanding one's rights as a citizen in the U.S., although there are innumerable instances wherein both amendments have been violated in the most hypocritical ways. For example, according to Wilkerson v. Utah, 99 U.S. 130 (1878), the U.S. Supreme Court ruled that public dissection, burning alive, drawing & quartering, or disemboweling is cruel and unusual punishment and should be avoided regardless of the crime. Just two years later, journalist/activist Ida. B. Wells found that at least 728 American African men and women had recently been lynched by White mobs who were never convicted nor punished for their crimes against humanity.

In more recent times, Supreme Court Justice Brennan found it necessary to set more judicial precedence regarding cruel and unusual punishment when he declared in Furman v. Georgia, 408 U.S. 238 (1972) that there are four principles used to determine cruel and unusual punishments:

1. The "essential predicate" is "that a punishment must not by its severity be degrading to human dignity," especially torture.
2. A severe punishment that is obviously inflicted in wholly arbitrary fashion.
3. A severe punishment that is clearly and totally rejected throughout society.
4. A severe punishment that is patently unnecessary.

One could cite the unfair sentencing laws for those charged with possession with intent to distribute "crack" as compared to those facing the same charges for cocaine. This example is interesting for several reasons, two of which we shall briefly address. The first is that the racial demographics for those distributing large amounts of cocaine is typically not an American African, but usually someone of a Spanish speaking population and/or a White individual. The second is the fact that "crack" actually contains less cocaine than the equal weight of cocaine (due to the fact that other ingredients are added to cocaine to make "crack"), yet the sentence, in some cases is ten times longer.

The racial injustice is blatant and is part of the politics of neglect carried-over from Woodson's time. It is very interesting to know how deeply engrained in the education process racism has become. To manipulate information towards producing a desired outcome is perhaps one of the most effective means of mis-educating. Woodson notes that:

> ...thousands and thousands of Negro children in this country [were] not permitted to use school books in which are printed the Declaration of Independence or the Constitution of the United States. (p. 83)

He further recalls a situation wherein a bill to have the U.S. Constitution printed in school history books was:

> ...killed by some one who made the point that it would never do to have Negroes study the Constitution of the United States. If the Negroes were granted the opportunity to peruse this document, they might learn to contend for the rights therein guaranteed; and no Negro teacher who gives attention to such matters of the government is tolerated in those backward districts. The teaching of government or the lack of such instruction, then, must be made to conform to the policy of "keeping the Negro in his place." (p. 83-84)

It's most interesting that many non-White students have an aversion to the study of U.S. History in elementary and secondary schools. There are many who mentally drop out of class when they begin to learn of the heroic presidents and the nobility of the Founding Fathers; albeit unconscious to most, there is a sense of dissonance that arises when one is forced to celebrate the likes of those who once enslaved their Ancestors and visited heinous crimes upon their souls. Some say it is akin to a Semite of the Jewish religion being told of the great and noble Adolf Hitler and his triumphs across the continent of Europe…this would never happen and if it did, would surely not be acceptable.

The "catch 22" for American African citizens of the U.S. is that one is "obligated" to celebrate the political figures of this country, especially those who are considered the founders. The general and usually unexpressed feeling is that to stray from this script could prove fatal due to the possibility of being labeled and treated as a domestic terrorist. On the other hand, there are large numbers of White Americans who openly threaten, slander, disrespect, and voice their disagreement with the current president, Barack Obama (who happens to be an American African) with little to no consequence.

While imprisoned on the plantations, the major tool for ensuring the enslavement of the minds of Africans was violence and religion; post-emancipation, it is/was violence, religion, and the classroom. It is within this context that children are given their location in history, complete with references to prior achievements and future possibilities. This is often done first and foremost through socialization, then in the subjects of history and politics. Unfortunately, few American African educators clearly recognize the power of a political education for their students; even fewer recognize the relationship between political and historical information and its impact on the self-esteem and identity of the same.

Woodson states:

> It was well understood that if by the teaching of history the White man could be further assured of his superiority and the Negro could be made to feel that he had always been a failure and that the subjection of his will to some other race is necessary, the freedman, then, would still be a slave. (p. 84)

The psychological impact of an authority figure promoting lies as if they are the truth is deep and yet to be fully discovered. It is due to this systemic mis-education that many individuals were incapable of achieving beyond their status as a slave. For those who did excel beyond the physical and mental imprisonment, they were almost always made aware of their Ancestral contributions to the erection of civilization in both the ancient and more recent past.

Woodson alludes to a phenomenon now called "The Willie Lynch Syndrome" in his perhaps most famous statement:

> If you can control a man's thinking you do not have to worry about his action. When you determine what a man shall think you do not have to concern yourself with what he will do. If you make a man feel that he is inferior you do not have to compel him to accept an inferior status, for he will seek it himself. If you make a man think that he is justly an outcast, you do not have to order him to the back door. He will go without being told; and if there is no back door, his very nature will demand one. (pp. 84-85)

A person trained and mis-educated into believing themselves unworthy of respect and opportunity is dealt a death sentence; a curse that will reach beyond the current generation deep into the future of their bloodline. It is a well-known fact in clinical and developmental psychology that a child's cognitive and identity development is in some degree a direct reflection of their primary caregivers and their immediate and most tangible environments. For the enslaved and recently emancipated African, this situation would almost guarantee their extinction. What also figures into the equation is the individual's personal and spiritual disposition. This last factor is what many psychological and African-centered scholars hold as the determining factor in the failure of systematic racism to totally annihilate the African from the known universe.

There are many people who have stated with amazement their disbelief that the African genotype remains active on the planet. This is a powerful testimony and is one that gives credence to a latent and determined factor held deep within the psyche of the African descendant. How is this potential actualized for a critical mass of Africans? How can this tool be consciously used to counteract the dumbing down process? In what ways can parents educate their children in order to awaken this power and raise the youth to mastery of self? Modern day African-centered "rites of passage" programs have been demonstrated to be effective at such a task, perhaps because they directly impact the world-view of the individual and assists in the restoration of a collective perspective within their family and community.

In light of this, Mr. Fuller provides a compensatory definition of "politics." He states that "politics" is any interaction between two or more people in any of the nine areas of people activity, including economics, education, entertainment, labor, law, religion, sex and war/counter war. The nature of a compensatory-based political education for American Africans, then would focus on how to best engage in interactions with others in a manner that 1) establishes justice, and 2) minimizes the conflict and potential for conflict. In a word, this is self-discipline and wisdom.

Since receiving a copy of the U.S. Constitution from Mr. Fuller, the author has read for himself the text of the 13th Amendment and has for the first time understood the relationship between the disproportionate incarceration of American African males and the maintenance of slavery and racism in this nation. The 13th Amendment reads:

> **Section 1.** Neither slavery nor involuntary servitude, *except as a punishment for crime whereof the party shall have been duly convicted* [emphasis added], shall exist within the United States, or any place subject to their jurisdiction.

To read this with an understanding of the large numbers of American Africans being incarcerated is one thing, but to include an analysis of popular culture that seemingly promotes behaviors that are likely to land one in prison is enough to startle even the most sound of minds. Many dismiss such a correlation as a conspiracy theory, which is actually true when conspiracy is defined as "a plot or plan carried out by two or more individuals."

Most recently, a song was released for radio play where a rapper, who is a former corrections officer, talks about smoking and selling dope on his cell phone. He explains throughout the song how he makes major drug transactions on his cellular phone and how he has a lot of business and leads a glamorous lifestyle based on these actions. There are other songs where the rappers promote violent and anti-social behaviors to their listening audience in repetitive fashion; when coupled with the videos, the message is reinforced through the use of operant conditioning, increasing the likelihood that the observers will participate in these criminal acts. The open assault on the potential for peaceful human interactions is a direct assault on having justice-based politics; and is only able to continue based on the mis-education of youth along the political lines.

The elimination of the Negro from politics, then, has been most unfortunate…To keep a man above vagabondage and crime he needs among other things the stimulus of patriotism, but how can a man be patriotic when the effect of his education is to the contrary?…***There are Negroes who know better, but such thinkers are kept in the background by the traducers of the race to prevent the enlightenment of the masses.*** [emphasis added](pp. 90, 94)

With this level of political disenfranchisement, coupled with the intentional criminalization of large segments of the race, American Africans are moving about blind to the reality of their situation. Priorities are determined by celebrities and tastes determined by marketing firms on Madison Avenue. Hopelessness and apathy are the passive order of the day, with little more than reactionary jerks to actions, which itself lasts but for a moment. The evidence of a lack of vision needs no further scrutiny…nonetheless, we shall proceed in the discussion via Woodson's next chapter *"The Loss of Vision."*

Chapter 10

Ignorance is Bliss
(The Loss of Vision)

*"We have appealed to the talented tenth for a remedy, but they
have nothing to offer. Their minds have never functioned in this
all-important sphere. The 'educated' Negro shows no evidence
of vision. He should see a new picture."*
Carter G. Woodson
The Mis-Education of the Negro

*"And art confident that thou thyself art a guide of the blind,
a light of them which are in darkness, An instructor of the
foolish, a teacher of babes, which hast the form of knowledge
and of the truth in the law."*
Romans 2:19-20 (KJV)

"In the land of the blind, the one-eyed man rules."
Proverb of Unknown Origins

The purposeful perpetuation of ignorance through the
withholding of factual, relevant, and pertinent information from
specific populations is a quick way to guarantee its demise.
Even more, when those who, against all odds, continue to
pursue enlightenment by seeking the truth and facts regarding
their reality, are publicly lynched (figuratively and literally)
and otherwise punished for their pursuits, others who fear the

same are encouraged towards docility and passivity. Eventually the standards for progress and the direction towards established goals become vague and less likely to rouse the defensiveness of the status quo.

In this situation, those who are subsequently elevated to the positions of leadership and those who are described as progressive and successful examples form the "glass ceiling" of character development, setting the bar relatively low in regards to what is truly necessary for any substantive change to actually take place. It becomes easy for the rhetorical and reactionary figure heads, arm chair activists, and wolves in sheep clothing to be given authority over the needs and desires of the people. As Dr. Woodson stated, "he easily learns to follow the line of least resistance rather than battle against odds for what real history has shown to be the right course" (p. 96). This type of deceptive leadership eventually culminates in a loss of "moral courage" and the American African will eventually "champion the cause of the oppressor" (p. 96).

In 1933, Woodson compared the American African of his time with those of the 18th century and found them wanting as far as their conviction and willingness to draw clear lines regarding their stance and position on the over-throwing of oppressive systems and situations. Today, the "moral surrender," as he called it, is perhaps beyond what Dr. Woodson could have imagined less than 80 years ago. This is due, in part, to the time and space that now separates modern American Africans from the relatively recent experiences of the plantation and the wicked oppression of chattel enslavement.

Some even suggest that modern American Africans have more to lose, and thus, are less likely to engage in thoughts, speech, and/or actions that will jeopardize the "progress" the race has achieved since emancipation. This would be an option for true consideration if there were not widespread and large-scale buffoonery in almost every aspect of American African entertainment and social systems (including our fraternities/sororities, educational institutions, family units, communities, and businesses). This buffoonery in itself jeopardizes the progress of American Africans through the presentation of living stereotypes that will substantiate the beliefs of inferiority about the American African.

Somehow, having a clear perspective of the source of one's hardship promotes the conjuring of a viable solution or at-least action and thinking towards that solution. Hence the value and necessity of maintaining the dumbing down process of large portions of respective populations.

> A mind that remains in the present atmosphere never undergoes sufficient development to experience what is commonly known as thinking. No Negro thus submerged in the ghetto, then, will have a clear conception of the present status of the race or sufficient foresight to plan for the future; and he drifts so far toward compromise that he loses moral courage. The education of the Negro, then, becomes a perfect device for control from without. Those who purposely promote it have every reason to rejoice, and Negroes themselves exultingly champion the cause of the oppressor. (p. 96)

Systematically rendered ineffective and for all intents and purposes incapable of effecting one's own liberation (mentally and physically), the American African has been rendered non-consequential (in regards to their ability to apply sufficient pressure, on a large enough scale, to bring about social and institutional change on a national and international level). This is not a hopeless death sentence, but a clue as to where the scattered energies of American Africans can be focused if perhaps, one day, the race will see freedom, justice, and equality as a norm and the perpetual and systematically enforced "niggerdom" banished into the annals of history as something to "never again" be revisited.

Thomas Burrell in his book *Brainwashed* identified the phenomenon in which American Africans rally behind international and distant causes, oft times spending large amounts of resources and energies towards publicizing their participation in international forums or those national issues that may garner copious amounts of media attention. This is done to the neglect of those issues taking place on their block or around the corner or in a neighboring community. Another important factor pointed out by Mr. Burrell is that many of these issues pertain to White on Black violence, while those that involve Black on Black violence are all but ignored.

What would happen if we took the example of Harriet Tubman who was reported to have carried two weapons: one for the oppressor and the other for the oppressed who served as extensions of the oppressor? What if all the Killers, Hip Hop Hustlers, and Super Slaves as defined by Raymond Winbush in *The Warrior Method* were called to task and forced to face a dissatisfied population of men, women and children who were tired of following the examples provided by these visionless, mindless and lifeless zombies? What if a critical mass decided to unplug and refuse the misguidance provided by those who have appointed themselves or have been elevated as plantation overseers of their own kind? The tables would surely turn.

Unfortunately, as stated by Woodson, it seems that these forms of resistance were more likely to have occurred here in the United States immediately after emancipation than at any other time since. One era that approaches this level of outright resistance was the Civil Rights Era, wherein American African and European American women and men displayed open defiance and complete dissatisfaction with the systems of racism and White supremacy maintained systematically in this nation. These cycles of increase and decline in resistance to oppression seem to be directly related to how clear and obvious the forms of oppression are to its victims. Another strong factor is how unified the oppressed populations are in regards to their internally determined needs and desires as it relates to their own situation.

Woodson provides examples of large numbers of American Africans who had been emancipated but refused to be deported to Liberia as well as those individuals he acknowledges for fighting against Jim-Crowism by courageously questioning the justness of a system wherein "one man has the prerogative to define rights for another." Today we have equally courageous activists, scholars, politicians, educators and spiritual leaders who fear not and consistently speak truth to power. At the same time, we have those who continue to consistently discredit the need for the identification, naming and framing of the problems facing the American African by American Africans. These detractors tend to use labels such as "reverse racism," "radical," and "militant" to cast a negative light on all things involving movement towards an oppression-free society constructed on the foundations of justice.

American Africans along with their White counterparts continue to be mis-educated in a system that claims the superiority of the latter over the inferior nature of the former. This equally creates confusion amongst both groups and encourages Whites and American Africans to maintain their discriminatory practices that benefit Whites and injures American Africans. It also causes American Africans to expect lower standards and treatment consistent with their "lowly" lot in life. This particular manifestation of racism/White supremacy is at the core of phenomena such as "White flight," segregation, and all forms of brutality visited upon non-White populations globally.

The systematic implications of such false beliefs and their subsequent actions are wide and highly varied. For example, much of the acceptance of substandard housing (lead-based paint and highly contaminated living environments), economic situations (predatory lending, credit denial), employment opportunities (denied job opportunities, workplace discrimination), political involvement (voting rights violations), basic human and civil rights (health care, food, clothing & shelter) are based on an inherent belief of inferiority implanted into the psyche of the oppressed population.

> And thus goes segregation which is the most far-reaching development in the history of the Negro since the enslavement of the race. In fact, it is a sequel of slavery. It has been made possible by our system of mis-educating innocent people who did not know what was happening. It is so subtle that men have participated in promoting it without knowing what they were doing...

> Although nominally free they have never been sufficiently enlightened to see the matter other than as slaves. One can cite cases of Negroes who opposed emancipation and denounced the abolitionists. A few who became free re-enslaved themselves. A still larger number made no effort to become free because they did not want to disconnect themselves from their masters, and their kind still object to full freedom. (p. 102)

A protective "barrier" of sorts is thus constructed to keep the destructive results of oppression, in the form of racism, from being observable by those who would much rather perpetuate it in silence and pretend they are not. Much like the "wall" of Wall Street constructed to block the view of the river upon which enslaved Africans were being unloaded and loaded on and off of ships for future sale at the auction block there in New Amsterdam (New York) or in another part of the spreading empire.

It's a sort of social and political quarantine, wherein the humanity and nobility of Africans has been systematically and intentionally destroyed and replaced by the infectious agent of European grown and cultivated "niggerdom." This population is then isolated and kept to itself in order that its perpetual and isolated influence is more likely to continue to auto-infect the population until eventually, adaptation, accommodation and assimilation occurs; installing "niggerdom" as a viable and "normal" part of the personality of the race. Furthermore, it prevents, or at best makes it extremely difficult for the developing mind to be exposed to thoughts, ideas, concepts, behaviors and various modes of functioning to challenge and move them beyond their current situation.

It is of the utmost importance that those who have been educated and who have achieved a station in life beyond that of a disempowered plantation prisoner (slave) or an ignorant and hate-filled plantation warden (slave-owner), find the ability to co-determine a plan of action for remedying the ill effects of racism and other forms of oppression. There needs to be "closed-door" meetings held amongst each of these groups to discuss what each will do to effect change in the direction of establishing justice in their daily lives. It is necessary for the American African to build up their confidence in their own ability to thrive as viable human beings with natural gifts and talents beyond those of their enslaved past. The vision necessary for this type of revolution is not easy to grasp by one who is so timid and fearful that they would rather maintain comfort as the foot-stools of society; but is reserved for those who reject fear for the more noble expressions of confidence, vigilance, and determination.

It would be equally as wrong for the newly found collective energies to be used by American Africans to establish oppressive systems and institutions directed towards the disempowerment of Whites and other populations. All energies should be directed towards the establishment of justice. Which simply means being fair, in reward and punishment, to all.

> Our minds must become sufficiently developed to use segregation to kill segregation…If the Negro in the ghetto must eternally be fed by the hand that pushes him into the ghetto, he will never become strong enough to get out of the ghetto. This assumption of Negro leadership in the ghetto, then, must not be confined to matters of religion, education, and social uplift; it must deal with such fundamental forces in life as make these things possible. (pp. 109-110)

The thrust must be towards making ourselves more viable by the steady, constant, and consistent improvement of ourselves as human beings; as an injured group needing to heal from the experiences of enslavement and continued oppression. We must developmentally go back and exchange our inferiority for the personality construct of industry as defined by Erik Erikson. We must revisit our developmental processes and be courageous enough as adults to correct our childhood traumas and mishaps, and subsequently, as parents enhance the programs we have laid out for our children. It is imperative, if one is to reach the long desired experience of justice, and to become self sufficient by enhancing their ability to produce those things that they themselves need for survival; effectively breaking the perpetual cycle of consumerism and dependency.

This is of course more than a notion and will require many steps to fulfill, nonetheless it is obtainable. Dr. Woodson recommends as a viable next step that the American African begin to value the role of service over that of leadership, so that fewer orders are given and more work is actually being done. He elaborates wonderfully in his next chapter *"The Need For Service Rather Than Leadership."*

Chapter 11

Words Without Works…
(The Need For Service Rather Than Leadership)

"In spite of its meager rewards, however, the idea of leadership looms high in the Negro mind. It always develops thus among oppressed people."

Carter G. Woodson
The Mis-education of the Negro

"Living on the frontline 'cuz ain't no room in the back…"
- Rossi Turner

Imagine, if you will, a third grade classroom. The teacher has just asked for a volunteer to assist with passing out cupcakes to the rest of the class…the classroom erupts with excitement as hands fly into the air, waving frantically to become the "chosen one." This "one," selected above all others, has the opportunity to break from the normal program and is allowed to distribute the much-desired goods to their peers. To look into the begging eyes of those not chosen, if only for the moment, grants total superiority to the "one." They all submit in order to ensure that they too will receive a treat. This is only part of the pleasure received by the selected assistant. The other part is the feeling of worth that may be otherwise absent in the day-to-day experiences of the children in this example.

For third graders, the above scenario is appropriate and usually without any major consequence. Of course the teacher may show favoritism and the child may be disproportionately chosen over the others. This may lead to some low-level "hating," which is, for the most part without significant consequence. But what of the adult that carries on in a similar fashion? What if instead, this were the scene at an HBCU (Historically Black College & University), and instead of 8 and 9 year old children, we are speaking about American African adults with advance degrees (M.D.s, Ph.D.s, Master's degrees, etc.) in a wide variety of disciplines including Physics, Psychology, Education, Public Health, English, etc. And what if, instead of cupcakes, these individuals were jockeying for the position of disseminating knowledge and information, as well as research funds, to the masses that are "dependent" on them for the latest information. And if instead of a classroom teacher, the center of attention was a major grant provider or funding source.

Just like the child who was selected to pass out the cupcakes, the professionally educated American African who is selected now has the "power" to decide how the monies, information, and duties will be distributed amongst those who desire to partake in the prize. Just as the child will select and choose those cupcakes with the most sprinkles, icing, and size for their close friends and give the "left-over" less attractive cupcakes to those they do not favor, the mis-educated American African will also be sure to award those whom they believe will follow their demands without questioning or challenging, those who will not make them feel insecure about their perceived power and authority, and those who they assume will make them look good in the end. And just like the child with the cupcakes, the professional American African must return to their "proper" place, once the short-lived empowerment has passed. Dr. Llaila Afrika often refers to this type of mis-educated American African as "certified Negroes under warranty."

This scene is so common that it may be statistically normal, but will forever be socially and culturally awkward. There are unfathomable numbers of professional and personal relationships that have been dissolved due to the mistreatment of a colleague for the sake of maintaining a position of power over others, even at the expense of the program. Professional American Africans who follow this mode of mis-education have literally and legally jeopardized entire institutions based on "knee-jerk" and impulsive decisions being made regarding trivial matters.

A mis-educated American African who has tasted what they perceived to be power is akin to a dog who has tasted blood. They become ultra territorial, their insecurities rise to the surface calling for a hyper-vigilant approach to all others, and perhaps most amazingly, all their degrees are instantly dumbed down to the social and cognitive level of the third graders mentioned above.

Woodson states:

> He is restricted in his sphere to small things, and with these he becomes satisfied. His ambition does not rise any higher than to plunge into the competition with his fellows for these trifles. At the same time those who have given the race such false ideals are busy in the higher spheres from which Negroes by their mis-education and racial guidance have been disbarred. (p. 111)

If not for the petty bickering and emotionally driven pre-mature dismissal of a colleague's insights, genuine willingness to contribute high-quality efforts to the program, and the fear associated with another's competence, the subsequent low quality final product could have easily become the industry standard or "best practice." In other words, the F.E.A.R. (False Evidence Appearing Real) associated with mis-education and dumbing down is one that debilitates and stagnates to the point that seemingly competent American Africans repeatedly produce products that unintentionally support the racist notions and stereotypes, relegating things produced by non-Whites to a substandard position.

> The selfish struggle for personal aggrandizement, which has not yet brought either faction more than an appointment on the police force or a clerkship in one of the city offices, thus blocks the social and economic progress of thousands. (p. 114)

All of this occurs while the teacher sits back and snickers to herself, while she looks on in amusement at how the children so readily compete for something so simple, yet so dear, as the prospect of passing out her cupcakes. While NIH, NIMH, Robert Woods Johnson Foundation, Ford, Kellogg and other well known funders are engaged in think tanks and meetings to determine what pursuits are important and hence, fundable, the professional yet dumbed down American Africans sit anxiously awaiting the next RFP (Request For Proposal) or RFA (Request for Application) to determine what they will be working on for the next couple of years and how much money they will have in their budgets. Meanwhile, the masses continue on with their "real" issues and problems that are of practical importance to both groups, without so much as a glance from those in the "Ivory Towers" of academia.

> This comes as a natural result, however, for the "education" of the Negro requires it. The ambitious mis-educated Negro in the struggle for the little things allotted by others prevents any achievement of the people in matters more constructive. Potentially the colored people are strong although they are actually weak.
>
> This much-ado-about nothing renders impossible cooperation, the most essential thing in the development of a people. The ambitious

of this class do more to keep the race in a state of turmoil and to prevent it from serious community effort than all the other elements combined. (pp. 112-113)

The competition for the self-appointed role of "leader" is nauseating and totally destructive. This single goal of becoming a leader symbolically represents an underlying desire to become powerful, respected, and capable of being self-sufficient. The position of leader has become synonymous with a power broker or one who accumulates the resources of the masses and distributes it as they see fit. There once existed a perspective that defined leadership as a role of service to those who selected the leader. It was not so much a glorious position, but instead, one heavy with responsibility, sacrifice, and oft times a sense of bondage to the people to whom one was accountable. In the latter example of leadership, they are often selected as opposed to being self-appointed, and tend to have demonstrated qualities making them fit to serve in the role.

In a conversation with scholar Camara Jules Harrell, this author earned a very enlightening and powerful understanding of the decline of the African state and leadership. Harrell, speaking of Ayi Kwei Armah's _Two Thousand Seasons_, shared the notion that African nations began to decline once rulership became based on inheritance rather than merit. The leadership that is gained through merit, in this context, includes the demonstration of higher mental, social, physical and spiritual capabilities; all of which will serve those who have chosen to follow. In the case of inherited leadership, the ruling class need not demonstrate nor aspire towards any level or semblance of nobility. Neither do they have to worry about their reign being legally challenged. The inherited model is not always a bad thing, but tends to be based on the family's own pride and integrity as it regards leadership and their role, responsibility, and obligations to society and the world as a whole.

In today's context of "democratically-driven" elections, candidates need only have a brilliant campaign, which the masses know and expect to be full of lies, false impressions and representations, in order to win. This comes with an abundant cash flow to fund tours, media products (radio and television commercials), and other items necessary to produce such an event. This method of persuasion is not very different from the one used by our highly trained officials in the pulpit who utilize this same type of appeal to recruit and retain the members of their congregation.

Leaders of another type have recently been given front stage in the lives of the masses. They show up in the popular culture as role models and present the world with their priorities. Athletes, actors, musicians, politicians, and other publicly popular and famous individuals usually occupy this class of leaders; backed by multi-billion dollar industries that tag along like a parasitic fish clinging to a shark, hoping to catch some of the scraps. As a side note, it is interesting how in these days there are social media products that literally carry the slogan "Follow Me"; a statement that is now widely used and adhered to with little regard to the character of the person being followed and the direction they are to take their subscribers.

An age-old tactic for oppressing and manipulating a mass of people dissimilar to the oppressor is to recruit from within the oppressed population for one to serve as a "middle-man." On the plantation of enslavement, it was the African overseer; in today's society, the highly mis-educated American African in the form of politicians, preachers, teachers, college professors, law enforcement, financial advisors, etc. have gladly transitioned into this role. The placing of such leaders amongst the population to be oppressed is for the purpose of maintaining direct influence and control, albeit from a distance, which also provides a buffer and the illusion of innocence on the part of the true oppressor, while making the oppression appear to be occurring at the hands and will of these appointed leaders.

> This was accomplished in the days of slavery by restricting the assembly of Negroes to certain times and places and compelling them to meet in the presence of a stipulated number of the "wisest and discreetest men of the community." The supervisors of the conduct of Negroes would prevent them from learning the truth which might make them "unruly" or ambitious to become free.

> After the Negroes became free the same end was reached by employing a Negro or some White man to spy upon and report behind closed doors on a plan to enslave the Negroes' minds. In case that actual employment as a spy seemed too bold, the person to be used as such an instrument took up some sort of enterprise which the oppressors of the race warmly supported to give him the desired influence in the community. This "racial racketeer" might be a politician, minister, teacher, director of a community center, or head of a "social uplift agency." As long as he did certain things and expressed the popular opinion on questions he lacked nothing, and those who followed him found their way apparently better paid as the years went by. (p. 116)

Just like the African overseers who were coerced and forced to torture and abuse their fellow plantation prisoners, the "overseer" of today will often "lose their soul" as a defense mechanism designed to separate their humanity from their minds and bodies, hence their actions. Thus, they are fully capable of delivering hardship, painful, immoral and unethical practices to their own people. The immediate threat of punishment in the form of economic hardship or physical pain/ death, simultaneously creates a need for immediate solutions or at least the illusion of a solution.

This condition creates a population wherein very few dare to think and even fewer dare to challenge the actions and proposals of the leadership. The ability to delay gratification, in order to think and ponder over matters before making decisions, is being made more difficult by the advent of more and more technology that cuts down on time and space between questions and answers, effectively training the human mind to expect all answers to come at the push of a button (i.e., Google), and for responses to inquiry to come via instant message or text.

As mentioned by Woodson, the resolve of this issue of leadership is not to be found in the continued abuse of the oppressive leadership. It will not serve the masses well to "waste their energy abusing those who misdirect and exploit them" (p. 117), but instead they should direct their energies towards identifying and protecting themselves from the various ways in which they are being manipulated, exploited and oppressed. Once this information is learned and disseminated, then the group must plan accordingly in order to secure their position beyond the will and influence of the oppressor.

Another survival tactic identified by Woodson is to be mindful of where financial support is given. He cautions the reader to thoroughly examine the details of solicitations for support in order to identify potential deception and long term issues that may not be apparent in the beginning. This piece of sound advice is applicable across the nine areas of people activity and would prevent a large amount of regret currently visited upon those who impulsively and emotionally lend their resources without proper scrutiny.

A recent example of highly-unscrutinized solicitation is during the tragic events occurring in New Orleans in the aftermath of Hurricane Katrina and more recently in Haiti following the devastating earthquake. Hundreds of groups solicited monies to "support" those in need in both of these disaster zones. Some well-intentioned donors later lamented when they realized the sham and that their funds never reached the intended destination.

At a very deep level, the "need" for leadership and the concurrent passivity involved while "waiting" for that leader to appear can be traced to the indoctrination and imposition of the European versions of Christianity on the enslaved and colonized Africans around the world. If one would research Arius and the Council of Nicea and the development of the Nicene Creed, it will become apparent that much of what is currently held as Christian belief concerning Jesus is at odds with what was originally held by Africans of similar faith. Arius, representing an Ancient African perspective of God, salvation, savior, leadership and individual empowerment served as the thorn in the side of "the church" at that time, with his message that ALL people had the right, responsibility and privilege of liberating themselves and redeeming their own spirits via their own efforts.

> ...the race will free itself from exploiters as soon as it decides to do so. No one else can accomplish this task for the race. It must plan and do so for itself. (p. 117)

Instead, what we have are masses of Africans, worldwide, who are patiently and passively awaiting their savior's return to liberate them from their current oppression and hardship. Many also believe that there is a curse that has been enacted by God Almighty upon those who have in someway and somehow disobeyed God's directions and teachings. This attitude of "deserving to be punished" equally serves the purpose of the oppressor and makes the oppressed more compliant with their current conditions. This is not an attack on Christianity, but a nudge to all Christians to examine more closely the origins of their current beliefs and its effects on their current status. Many of our church leaders know this information, yet, will not expound upon it in any meaningful way in the presence of their congregations. This keeps the people as "sheeple" (sheep + people = blind herd of humans), waiting for their leader's message, and their saviors return. Meanwhile, obesity, divorce, drug and alcohol abuse, crime, illness, violence, deception, and economic hardship continue to visit the flock.

> When you hear a man talking, then, always inquire as to what he is doing or what he has done for humanity…It may be well to repeat here the saying that old men talk of what they have done, young men talk of what they are doing, and fools of what they expect to do. The Negro race has a rather large share of the last mentioned class. (p. 118)

The eventual shift from a leadership-dependent state-of-mind to one of service and a more industrious attitude must be at the core of any efforts to improve the condition of American Africans and all people as a whole. There is nothing more capable of boosting the self-esteem and sense of efficacy of a developing child like a task completed successfully. And no task is approached with more enthusiasm than those that are chosen by the workers themselves.

Therefore, it becomes the responsibility of our current, able-minded and physically capable citizens to begin to construct opportunities designed to boost a desire to think, work, construct, alter, and produce for one's self. The rewards for such a transition may not be immediate, but will definitely be long lasting and invaluable to those who so choose to live.

To once again have that desire to do for self as exemplified by two-year-old toddlers who literally throw tantrums if someone does for them what they desire to do for self; or if for just a few generations, the idea of leadership were redefined to reflect that of servitude and equal opportunity to make a worthy contribution, there would surely be a turn around in the prognosis of the American African as an oppressed population.

> Under leadership we have come into the ghetto; by service within the ranks we may work our way out of it. Under leadership we have been constrained to do the biddings of others; by service we may work out a program in the light of our own circumstances. Under leadership we have become poverty-stricken; by service we may teach the masses how to earn a living honestly. Under leadership we have been made to despise our own possibilities and to develop into parasites; by service we may prove sufficient unto the task of self-development and contribute our part to modern culture. (p. 119)

Until such a change becomes reality, there will continue to be "*Heirlings in the Places of Public Servants*," deceiving and manipulating those being served into believing they are benefitting from their continued oppression.

Chapter 12

Gatekeepers and Tokens
(Hirelings in the Place of Public Servants)

"...but the bulk of the work of raising the Negro must be done by the Negro himself, and the greatest help for him [from Whites] will be not to hinder and curtail and discourage his efforts. Against prejudice, injustice and wrong the Negro ought to protest energetically and continuously, but he must never forget that he protests because those things hinder his own efforts, and that those efforts are the key to his future...And those efforts must be mighty and comprehensive, persistent, well-aimed and tireless; satisfied with no partial success, lulled to sleep by no colorless victories; and, above all, guided by no low selfish ideals; at the same time they must be tempered by common sense and rational expectations."

W.E.B. Du Bois
The Philadelphia Negro

The role of the public servant is simply to serve the public, specifically those within one's own jurisdiction or community. There are many public servants who genuinely have the altruistic drive to be the voice of the people, negotiating the political and legal systems on their behalf, teaching and administering in academic institutions, providing health services in local clinics and hospitals, providing safety and security to neighborhoods and communities, and ministering around religious and spiritual matters. Equally, there are those who are simply put into place by the powers that be in order to maintain the status quo and to manipulate the masses towards their continued oppression by mis-educating, participating in unethical and unjust legal and medical practices, unfair punishment, patrolling and implementation of the law, as well as pulpit pimping. These are called hirelings and have been referred to as "wolves in sheep's clothing," "Uncle Toms" (although this is an incorrect labeling because Uncle Tom in the famous story was actually quite revolutionary), "sell-outs," "over-seers," and other unpleasant terms used to describe American Africans who seem to be doing the bidding of an oppressive system.

These hirelings may be found in all walks of life and in modern times have become more sophisticated in their disguise and performance. The degree of sophistication has served several purposes, namely, to make it more difficult to identify a hireling, and also to make it easier to misidentify a "true" public servant as a hireling. The confusion created around this issue is marvelous. In a situation where ignorance is held in high esteem while success and educational attainment are labeled as "acting White," it is of little surprise that those who champion the social, academic, and cultural uplift of American Africans often receive the labels associated with hirelings. Stated differently, it is not surprising that those who aspire towards academic excellence, moral and ethical character traits, and economic stability, are often considered to be sell-outs, uncle toms, and acting White. In contrast, individuals who glamorize the continued oppression and ignorance of the race are considered to be "keeping it real" and receive the highest levels of "street cred" (credibility amongst the masses).

It is amazing how easy the progress of American Africans is stifled by trivial confusions and misidentification, which may ultimately escalate to the level of street wars amongst rival gangs, "rival" liberation groups, "rival" religious groups, and even "rival" sororities and fraternities. This type of petty rivalry can be seen throughout the liberation movements manufactured by and on behalf of American Africans and Africans elsewhere in the Diaspora. For example, the "beef" between Booker T. Washington and W.E.B. Du Bois, or the "beef" between Marcus Mosiah Garvey and W.E.B. Du Bois, or even the "beef" between Malcolm X and Martin Luther King, Jr., all were counterproductive and would have better served their respective communities if they were annulled. In each of these cases, there were harsh words exchanged and less than beneficial perspectives shared publicly about one another, which ultimately kept their followers unnecessarily confused and divided.

Imagine if instead of Malcolm X referring to Martin Luther King, Jr. as a hireling, or if instead of Garvey calling Du Bois a hireling, they saw how each perspective was valid and had its place in the upliftment of the American African. If only each perspective could more easily and confidently identify the other as a "true" public servant. If only each group could realize and respect that the "followers" of one "leader" have their work to do and their own contributions to make, and that these advances serve only to uplift the whole, posing no threat to the path of another. This is like your circulatory system "beefing" with your digestive system because its sole focus is breaking down food and preparing nutrients for distribution throughout the body.

The circulatory system, in this hypothetical scenario, believes that all aspects of the body should be as focused and devoted as it is to the work of transporting the blood throughout the body. The fact is that both are totally dependent on each other, for without the work of the digestive system, the nutrient value of the blood would be virtually non-existent.

Likewise, without the circulation of the blood, the cells and tissues of the digestive system would suffer because they themselves would be undernourished; not to mention, there would be no way for the stomach to distribute its substance beyond the intestinal tract without the blood.

An excellent and more recent example of this sort of "beef" is between Dr. Karenga's US Organization and the Black Panther Party, via Bunchie Carter. This one literally ended in bloodshed and the loss of a great community organizer. It was later determined that the FBI's Counter Intelligence Program (Co-Intel Pro) assisted in the orchestration of this "beef" wherein the methods of the US Organization and Karenga's focus on the cultural, spiritual, character and intellectual upliftment of Africans was labeled that of "arm-chair revolutionaries" (hirelings). In every one of these cases, the approach and perspectives of each group were different, but the goal was similar and directly motivated by the desire to end the oppression of American Africans and install justice in its place.

> The strong have always used this as a means of dealing with the so-called weaker races of the world. The Caucasian arrays the one against the other so that they may never combine their forces and thus deprive their so-called superiors of control over them, which they could easily do if organized. One White man was thus able to maintain himself on a plantation where there were thirty or forty slaves because the Negroes were mis-educated in such a way as to keep them divided into distinct factions. In petty strife their power would be lost in the process of attrition. Today we find the same thing in Africa where his end is reached by embittering one tribe against another; and it worked the same way in India until recently when it began to break down under the masterful leadership of Mahatma Gandhi. (pp. 122-3)

Indeed, this "petty strife" has all but depleted the inner fire needed by American Africans to push forward and overcome, once and for all, the oppressive mind-state and environments bequeathed them by the process of enslavement and colonization. Spelled out very clearly within the pages of the now infamous *Willie Lynch Letter: The Making of a Slave* is the psychological process, based on the philosophy of behaviorism, underlying the future development of dissension, disorganization, and infantile bickering within a group of people who have more in common than not. Adults who potentially would and could be productive and progressive citizens and leaders of their communities are trapped by their inner child who unknowingly carries the trans-generational wounds of their ancestors who were never allowed to mature beyond physical servitude, while being forced to reproduce and "parent" offspring in their injured state. The cycle continues unchecked, unacknowledged, and without known or practical remedy.

The level of healing needed has never been totally determined. This is partially because the vastness and complete nature of the problem has yet to be determined. Meanwhile, the American African community continues along on auto-pilot, programmed by those who benefit most from their ignorant state. And the highly mis-educated American African is placed in the captain's chair and serves as much of a purpose as the inflatable "dummy" pilots seen in the *Airplane* movies of the 70s. These "captains" appoint their hirelings: co-pilots, flight attendants, and first class passengers; their friends, the people whom they can trust to keep the façade in tact, and who will quietly enjoy the crumbs from the master's table like roaches, while turning a blind eye on the suffrage of their fellow American Africans riding coach or being escorted off the plane by a prejudiced and overzealous TSA agent.

In the world of education, these are those who gain positions of influence but neglect to challenge their students and consumers to expect more from themselves and to produce above and beyond the mediocrity that is surrounding them. These people are either unwilling or incapable of putting education in its appropriate context, which, in turn assists with placing the true value and aim of educational pursuits well below its worth. This structure sets up a cycle not easily broken, but instead, one easily perpetuated due to the increasing numbers of individuals who have stakes in the façade and the raw motivation to maintain the illusion of progress. These are the individuals who are slowly creeping into positions of influence who may or may not have realized their own mis-education, but nonetheless, operate to support and maintain their benefits from the same.

The author recalls a conversation with a mentor while attending a conference in psychology for American African graduate students. The mentor, himself a researcher and scholar who studies the impact of racism on American African health, stated that many of the students at the conference were being trained (intentionally and unintentionally) to maintain the existing paradigm of White supremacy, and have as their direct mission the continued use of psychological tools as weapons to maintain an oppressed mentality in American Africans. The author's desire to contextualize education in order to prioritize those methods and research interests towards areas most relevant and pertinent to the psychological, spiritual, and cultural development of oppressed populations was not shared by these individuals.

This eerie statement presented very sincerely and with a troubling underlying message, served to make the author aware of the reality of mis-education. The statement demonstrated the intentional nature behind the dumbing down process, and how Kuhn's notions of the paradigm, how it is preserved and forced to shift, are played out most readily in the halls of academia; making frontline soldiers of the unsuspecting student.

Annually, there are thousands of American Africans who graduate from HBCUs and PWIs who haven't the slightest clue about the cultural and intellectual impact of the enslavement process. Many of these same persons will combat anyone who attempts to shed light on the legacy yet to be discovered. It becomes a risk to discuss things of this matter; even those who are the "talented tenth" and have joined American African Greek-lettered organizations and Masonic Lodges of Prince Hall Affiliation have yet to fully and totally embrace the African-centeredness (in principle) of their founders and earliest members.

As a professor, it is always surprising to the author how few students in institutions of higher education understand the climate in which their ancestors attended college, founded organizations, and challenged the status quo when it came to their rights. It is still taboo to discuss how significant it is for Martin Delany or W.E.B. Du Bois to have attended Harvard University during that era. Or for Prince Hall to have successfully challenged the then existing culture regarding the African worthiness of Brotherhood to the degree that he could start African Lodge #1, (later numbered 459) of Free and Accepted Masons as an attempt to reclaim, for his ancestors, their position as the original Worshipful Grand Masters, as did George G.M. James in _Stolen Legacy_.

In full agreement with Dr. Woodson, this author proposes that the most active "hirelings" occupy the classroom and pulpits as teachers, professors, and preachers. These aspects of society are the most heavily populated with "hirelings" because they are the very aspects of society that are best positioned for resurrecting the insightful and courageous spirit of the American African.

The Negroes' point of view, therefore, must be changed before they can construct a program which will bring them out of the wilderness. For example, no good can be expected from one of our teachers who said that she had to give up her class in Sunday school to accept an extra job of waiting on table at that hour because she had bought a twenty-four-hundred-dollar coat and her husband had purchased an expensive car. Such a teacher has no message for the Negro child. Her example would tend to drag the youth downward, and the very thought of having such a person in the schoolroom is most depressing.

We must feel equally discouraged when we see a minister driving up to his church on Sunday morning in a Cadillac. He does not come to feed the multitude spiritually. He comes to fleece the flock. The appeal he makes is usually emotional. While the people are feeling happy the expensive machine is granted, and the prolonged vacation to use it is easily financed. Thus the thoughtless drift backward toward slavery…No people can go forward when the majority of those who should know better have chosen to go backward, but this is exactly what most of our misleaders do. Not being learned in the history and background of the race, they figure out that there is no hope for the masses; and they decide, then, that the best thing they can do is to exploit these people for all they can and use the accumulations selfishly. Such persons have no vision and therefore perish at their own hands. (pp. 124-5)

So what of a community and a people lacking the influence of a visionary with a beneficial vision? From whence does their motivation, direction, and striving towards sustainable growth and improvement come? Is it possible for the hungry to lead the hungry to food if both individuals know not the direction or provider of their next meal? Is it possible for those who are visually impaired to lead those that are visually impaired across unfamiliar terrain? Of course it is. But will the journey be without its trials? Of course not. Will it be an efficient process whereby it is completed in a timely and direct fashion? Probably not. In fact, if left up to choice, most would choose a better option. Most would probably choose for themselves an option wherein they are empowered to navigate life in an efficient and effective manner; an option that removes the "handicap" from their being and levels the playing field, with equal opportunity for all. In short, an option that is just, with justice as its intention.

These questions are often entertained by American Africans who have considered segregation as opposed to de-segregation (not to be confused with integration), and by those who find themselves dissatisfied with the "progress" of the former plantation prisoner once called by many names (nigger, Black, African, African American, American African, minority, etc.). The notion of being led and needing vision is nothing new, it's only unique in the lives of American Africans because of the relatively short-lived (in relation to the vast history of African civilization), but deeply impactful experience of enslavement and colonization.

The question of "who speaks for the Negro," and what type of leadership is best and necessary has often led to disagreements and sometimes bloodshed (as outlined above). Many African nations have been propped up by the installment of "post-colonial" leaders who have (on many occasions) been identified as an ally of the previous colonial government, just as many American African organizations were infiltrated and eventually neutralized by externally planted internal strife.

> The enemies of the race, for example, will find a Negro willing to do certain things they desire to have accomplished and will finance him and give him sufficient publicity to get before the world, for the few favors which he may dispense among his followers…(p. 123)

With this in mind, it is not surprising that many Africans throughout the Diaspora have advocated for the total separation from the legacy of their enslavers and colonizers. Certain of their former enslavers simultaneously advocated for the same, although for very different reasons. It is often argued by those American Africans in favor of total separation that the only way to be free of the oppressive and racist influence of White supremacists, who formerly held them in bondage and currently maintain control of most aspects of society, is to return to Africa to live (repatriation); others of the same opinion offer the need for separate schools, neighborhoods, banks, professionals, etc., within the same community (segregation). Some even advocate for the allotment of massive amounts of land partitioned off for the use and benefit of the descendants of enslaved Africans as restitution (reparations). Regardless of the form of the separation, it all seems to be motivated by an inherent distrust and fear of Whites; a fear that is based on the ongoing and well-documented injustice and trauma experienced by non-Whites at the hands of Whites.

The desire of Whites for "total" separation seems to be rooted in the same emotion of fear, however, their fear tends to be more driven by the unknown possibilities of American Africans (or other oppressed populations) one day seeking to avenge their ancestor's suffering by reciprocating and returning the violence once visited upon them. It is similar to a situation where "person A" has stolen something from "person B" and is unsure if "person B" is aware of the transgression. The two must continue to interact with each other, all the while, "person A" is nervous, defensive, and definitely apprehensive towards "person B" based on their own guilt and knowledge of their actions. This may lead "person A" to incriminate "person B" in order to remove the "threat" from their environment.

Again, the entire scenario is based upon "person A" secretly committing a crime, and their subsequent feelings of guilt and fear associated with the *possibility* of "person B" becoming aware of the crime, and the potential for subsequent reactions in search of justice...hence the *need* for mis-education. The displacement of the criminal element onto the victim by the guilty party is a well-known manifestation of a psychological ego defense mechanism called projection. For example, the early and modern media images portraying American African males as rapist, thieves, and barbarous animals, and American African females as sex addicted breeders, is thought by many to be the European projecting onto Africans, the diabolical deeds that some Europeans and their descendants have visited upon Africans and other non-White populations.

It can't be reiterated enough that the insidious nature of racism makes it such that many are unaware of its continued ploys to maintain White superiority over non-White people.

> As we realize more and more that education is not merely imparting information which is expected to produce certain results, we see very clearly the inconsistency of the position of White persons as executives of Negro institutions…they are so far out of sympathy with the Negro that they cannot make any contribution to educational practice…It is all right to have a White man as the head of a Negro college or to have a red man at the head of a yellow one, if in each case the incumbent has taken out his naturalization papers and has identified himself as one of the group which he is trying to serve… The real servant of the people must live among them, think with them, feel for them, and die for them. (pp. 128-129)

As an educator, it is of the utmost importance to study the social, political, cultural, and economic implications of education. This will inherently provide for the perspective of education mentioned by Woodson above, carrying it beyond the notion of the simple provision of information to certain populations. It will eventually generate a perspective of education that includes how information presented through multiple forms of media impacts the learner in a multitude of ways. It will also reveal how the presentation of particular subjects (i.e., cultural history) can shape the self-concept and subsequently the self-esteem and self-efficacy of the student.

It is a true servant who is best capable of clearly identifying with those served, especially if they are, as Woodson stated, living among, thinking with, and feeling for them. This requirement of true servitude subtly points to an all important aspect of the leadership-servant dynamic, which is becoming ever more vacant in the American African experience, that is, the leadership and service provided by mature and emotionally capable parents. It is this author's belief that the family is perhaps the most detrimental place to have a hireling in the place of a servant, for it totally displaces the potential of the growing child and family unit.

It is within this structure that the personality of the individual is most heavily influenced and rendered either effective or ineffective. It is within this structure that one must find the remedy for centuries of dumbing down through the mis-education process. And it is from this point that we will launch our mission to delve deeper into the fundamental attributes of the American African and how this understanding can facilitate the development of a plan for correcting and preventing further dumbing down and oppression. Let us now reflect on Woodson's next chapter, and see how we must "*Understand the Negro.*"

Chapter 13

Overstanding the Situation
(Understand the Negro)

"And once you come to the full understanding that the angels are the sources of your talents, genius, health and well being, as well as ills, and that there has been a science stretching back into prehistory that teaches how to cultivate these parts of your being you will wonder why you haven't been taught the truth."

-Ra Un Nefer Amen
Metu Neter vol. 6

"**W**hat do you think of the statement 'emancipate yourselves from mental slavery none but ourselves can free our minds'?," asked a student of African studies at a prestigious HBCU.

"It is as applicable today as ever," replied the author, "except that it will surely take some spark from the outside to get things rolling in that direction…"

"So are you saying that Africans throughout the diaspora are incapable of resolving their own issues totally independent of those who are currently in control of their situations?," the student continued. To which the author provided the following response:

"If you would treat the current state of African consciousness as if it were somnambulism (sleepwalking), it may be easier to see what I mean. Many are drifting on autopilot without a clue of the fact that they are even drifting. There is so much going on beneath the threshold of consciousness that the real task in many situations is to get people to become aware of their movement (thoughts, attitudes, self-concept, speech and action). There is something that the oppressor knows about the oppressed that the oppressed does not consciously know about its Self. It is here that we would benefit from focusing our explorative energies."

"Are you saying that we need to ask the oppressor to help us out of our situation???," exclaimed the student.

"Not at all. What I *am* saying is that with all of the cultural, historical, and political information we have gathered to date, none of it has established justice nor has it returned the diasporic African to a place of sovereignty. Which logically, to me, means that there is something that we are missing; something that will render the tools of the oppressor less effective, while simultaneously creating a more efficient and effective African. When one studies the scientific processes utilized during the enslavement and colonization periods, it will become apparent that there was much energy directed towards the destruction and reconstruction of the African's awareness of its spiritual power, identity and personality."

"From the western psychological perspective, this was simply a function of the brain and behavior of the African. However, from the perspective of the Africans themselves, this was an assault to the spiritual nature and functionality of the African. This diabolical shift in the worldview (value system, epistemology, and ontology) of the African reshaped the information from which the mind is constructed, to reflect the limited and virtually dysfunctional personality desired and needed by the oppressors and their systems. Understanding this psycho-spiritual shift is the key to truly liberating the oppressed African and bringing them to their rightful place as sovereigns in their own rights, and hence, in the presence of the global community."

"As a researcher and scientist, the tool of observation is powerful, especially when coupled with the appropriate questions and the freedom to explore without the constraints of inherent and externally imposed limitations. Thus far, the majority of the knowledge-based quests for liberating information for the diasporic African has been in reaction to, or otherwise motivated by, the oppressor. Like in any good competition, the winning strategy is to keep the opponent thinking defensively as opposed to offensively. This approach keeps the oppressed in a reactionary and imbalanced state, making them less likely to think, plan and/or act beyond their current situations. In fact, the oppressed is 'forced' into a mode of operating that does not favor the delay of gratification, the development of patience, the use of deep protracted thinking, the saving of valuable resources, building (mentally and physically), and seeking stability. On the contrary, this mode of operating produces impulsive risk taking, temporary situations that are better if afforded some longevity, scattered loyalties, wasted resources, and a hampered desire for high quality interactions and character."

"To truly know what it will take to understand the potential of the oppressed populations is to find a period in time when those same populations were functioning outside of the influence of their current oppressors. Within this observational exercise, one would benefit greatly by finding various and varying perspectives, from a multitude of sources about a multitude of topics. Begin to explore those topics that have been labeled 'taboo' by the powers that be. Delve deeply into the belief systems of these once empowered nations. Identify those sources of strength that once existed but are absent now. Seek to recognize what was given to the oppressed by the oppressor and gather information about how those 'gifts' have served the oppressed."

"One would also do good on this quest to study certain psychological concepts including the ego defense mechanisms, classical and operant conditioning, as well as the notion of mental health and psychopathology. As mentioned by master teacher Neely Fuller, Jr. 'until one understands racism/White supremacy, what it is and how it functions, everything else you *think* you understand will only confuse you.'; with this, I strongly recommend making a deep study of racism and its only functional form which is White supremacy. Go beyond the economic explanations of enslavement and seek out the true motivating forces behind the brutal treatment of melaninated populations on a global scale by those who classify themselves as White. Seek out those records and first hand accounts, as documented by the oppressors themselves, regarding how they felt when faced with the issues of genetic survival."

"Please do not lock yourself into simply exploring what occurred yesterday (historically speaking), but instead, be as the Sankofa bird and draw the correlations between what you find has occurred in the past, its current manifestations, and future implications. Realize how susceptible the injured mind is to further influences from those who benefit from their crippled state. Analyze marketing, popular culture, fashion trends, and the purposeful production of incompetence through the rewarding of destructive imagery to certain populations while simultaneously monitoring and preventing the same to ever occur in reference to other populations. For example, certain rappers are able to discuss, without censor, the murdering, robbing, and destruction of other American Africans (commonly referred to as niggaz, niggers, etc.), while within the same song, references of the disabled, Jews, and the sexually diverse (i.e., homosexuals) are almost always muted or otherwise removed from the expression. Is it that these groups are more valuable than American Africans, and thus prevent such offenses from taking place? Or could it be that those responsible for censoring the media despise the American African to the degree that such assaults are not only allowed, but actually sought after and greatly rewarded? These are just questions to stimulate thought and action towards your goal."

As stated by Woodson:

> The chief difficulty with the education of the Negro is that it has been largely imitation resulting in the enslavement of his mind. Somebody outside the race has desired to try out on Negroes some experiment which interested him and his coworkers; and Negroes, being objects of charity, have received them cordially and have done what they required. In fact, the keynote in the education of the Negro has been to do what he is told to do. Any Negro who has learned to do this is well prepared to function in the American social order as others would have him. (p. 134)

"This experiment is what must be figured out. It seems to be some sort of mind control or 'zombification' of the African which has allowed them to, on one hand participate in the mutilation of their brothers and sisters as experienced under King Leopold's reign over the Belgian Congo, or the more modern violence experienced in the so-called ghettos via drug distribution and gang activities. In all of these examples, Africans are never the direct benefactor of the situation, nor are they the producers of the situation in-which they are found; and according to certain behaviorists, the situation is easily constructed and is known to manipulate and influence behaviors. For example, if an environment were kept in a "cold" temperature (i.e., restaurant) the customers who found the cold uncomfortable would spend less time in the facility, thus freeing up their seats for other waiting customers. A community laced with violence, crime, trash, very little natural landscape and large over-bearing buildings of stone, tend to restrict and limit mobility, thoughts and desires, as well as beget more violence, crime, trashing, and increased stagnation."

"As an individual interested in truly overstanding the current situation, it would be beneficial to explore one's own comfort with falsehood, deception and lies. It would be beneficial to also realize how you, yourself have been complacent and compliant with your own oppression. This will lead you to a similar conclusion as I have arrived at: that there is a need for something external to stimulate the sleepwalker awake. When asleep and dreaming, most do not realize that they were/are asleep until they wake up. Very few, aside from those who are specially trained to do so, realize the moment at which they actually fall asleep. Most function in dreams as if they are living in an awakened state and only realize it was 'just a dream' once they wake up. Sometimes even the heart beat, respiration, and sex organs are even fooled into action/ reaction by the experience."

"There are plenty of information-filled revolutionaries dying of obesity, lung cancer from smoking, liver disease from alcohol consumption, and other totally preventable situations. We have potentially great political servants and leaders who's careers are destroyed prior to its proper beginnings due to some 'youthful indiscretions' that may have been conveniently placed and brought up at the most opportune time. We now have hip hop artists who are elevated to the status of our greatest philosophers and activists for simply contributing a verse, a song, or maybe just a line that hints at social responsibility, while almost all other lyrics point unmistakably towards the destruction of their community and those like them. Why is there such a blatant denial of the African's role in the construction of civilization and their unquestionable contribution to the progress experienced by human beings of all nations and lands? Who would stand to suffer should all of these injustices be addressed and corrected? Who would benefit?"

> In this particular respect "Negro education" is a failure, and disastrously so, because in its present predicament the race is especially in need of vision and invention to give humanity something new. The world does not want and will never have the heroes and heroines of the past. What this age needs is an enlightened youth not to undertake the tasks like theirs but to imbibe the spirit of these great men and answer the present call of duty with equal nobleness of soul...their only hope is to know themselves and the generation they are to serve. The chief value in studying the records of others is to become better acquainted with oneself and with one's possibilities to live and to do in the present age...The most inviting field for discovery and invention, then, is the Negro himself, but he does not realize it. (pp. 138-9)

"Finally, I would like to suggest to you, that you take a look at the African as you would a piece of coal destined to become a diamond. Realize the pressure that is necessary to coerce the carbon bonds configured to produce coal into rearranging themselves in order to become one of the hardest materials known to humans, a diamond. With the centuries worth of oppression dealt to Africans, there just may be some higher level of influence that has helped the African to endure and continue to generate new methods of interacting with their ever-changing environments. Just like the coal, the African without the extreme external pressure was fully functional and a major contributor to the expansion of humanity. And just like that piece of coal, the pressured African can emerge with such brilliance that their contribution will once again be coveted and respected by the elite of the elite."

"Endurance and integrity seem to be what is required to move beyond the discomfort of our current situations. One must be forever courageous enough to explore those areas once forbidden by our oppressors via our social, religious, political and academic institutions. And in this exploration, one must develop a spirit of discernment in order to not mistake your jewels for rubbish and the rubbish for your jewels."

"Once you have given great consideration to the things mentioned in this conversation, we will be ready to begin constructing our *New Program.*"

Chapter 14

The New, New Program
(The New Program)

"The thing that hath been, it is that which shall be; and that which is done, is that which shall be done; and there is no new thing under the sun."

Ecclesiastes 1:9 (KJV)

"The program to uplift of the Negro in this country must be based upon a scientific study of the Negro from within to develop in him the power to do for himself what his oppressors will never do to elevate him to the level of others."

Carter G. Woodson
The Mis-education of the Negro

Much of what Dr. Woodson describes as the "new" program for American Africans is focused on the following two areas of interest: school-based education and organized religion in the form of the church. His discussion links the two as mutual factors used to determine the issues experienced by American Africans. He maintains that the religious, political, economic, and educational leadership as they existed in his time were produced by the system of mis-education. He maintains that the American African population was intentionally dumbed down in order to produce a class of "backwards" humans who would be helpless in the process of asserting themselves for their basic human rights. Woodson took the position that if the current system had produced such shadows of leadership, then it is the system that must be overhauled and refined as a part of the new program.

As regards education, Woodson identifies the following items as the most important tasks to be undertaken if one is to approach the establishment of justice here in the United States of America:

1. ***Teachers must revolutionize the social order for the benefit of the community.*** The reasoning behind this point is that those who are truly fit to teach are also those who are truly fit to lead those whom they are teaching. These individuals carry the responsibility of learning more about the people whom have been entrusted to their care, and to incorporate this new knowledge into their teaching styles.

2. ***More attention must be paid to the development of American Africans during the antebellum period in the form of deep, scientific, and multidisciplinary studies.*** The purpose of this proposition was to dispel the negative and derogatory myths associated with the character and intellectual capabilities of the American African recently freed from the plantation. It was Dr. Woodson's thesis that much of the intellectual, cultural, and social nuances that remained with the emancipated African were in fact, residual attributes that survived the brutality of enslavement. To identify such a transmission of culture serves the function of: 1) identifying the tremendous asset of resiliency possessed by the enslaved Africans, and 2) challenging the myth that Africans emerged from the enslavement process as an "ignoramus" and more animalistic than humane.

3. ***Higher education must be refined and redefined as "the preparation to think and work out a program to***

serve the lowly rather than to live as an aristocrat" (p. 149). This refinement and redefinition must focus mostly on the disciplines of theology, social work, psychology, education and literature. The remaining disciplines should be scrubbed of their racist subtleties that promote the inferiority of the African through so-called scientific proofs.

4. *No HBCU should be closed due to their proven ineffectiveness or inability to educate* according to the definition provided above, but instead, the entire "system" of HBCU's should be restructured to perform more efficiently and effectively for the upliftment of those who are less capable in their surrounding communities.

5. *The information disseminated at ALL academic institutions should be balanced out to include truthful and factual information about the contributions of all races and cultures involved in the subject matter.* For example, if teaching about George Washington, one should also include the numbers of African descendants who served alongside him during his battles. If teaching of the early Greek elite, speak also of the African sages from which the Greeks acquired much of their insight.

6. *American Africans enrolled in programs of higher education should be trained and prepared to identify those issues that are most important to their race and community* and should be encouraged and directed to seek solutions and programs to efficiently and effectively address their concerns.

In regards to the church and other religious institutions, Dr. Woodson proffers the following list of items to be addressed if there is to be the establishment of justice:

1. ***Religious institutions must get rid of leaders "who are not prepared to help the people whom they exploit"*** (p. 146). The people who follow such leadership must no longer tolerate the exploitative and hypocritical nature of such persons. The people must demand that those within these religious institutions, who are responsible for the creation of the current systems of education "be awakened, and if this is impossible they must be dethroned. Those who keep the people in ignorance and play upon their emotions must be exiled" (p. 146). For those religious leaders who survive the purging, they must begin to teach their followers the true meaning of religion and infuse them with the scientific and practical knowledge necessary for advancing their status as human beings. It is also of the utmost importance for these leaders to truly know their congregation in a personal and respectable manner.

2. ***Religious leaders must throw away the religion of their former oppressors and begin to "reinterpret" their respective religious systems in favor of establishing equality and justice amongst its followers.*** The revision of religious concepts and ideas is imperative for a group of disjointed and scattered people such as the formerly enslaved African. This, if carried out properly, would facilitate the unification of the otherwise segregated pockets of American Africans who feel that they ascribe to divergent religious perspectives, of which only theirs is correct and leads to salvation.

3. ***These religious institutions must reduce their numbers in regards to its supervisory staff.*** Such large numbers "at the top" can easily become a financial burden, or at best a distraction away from more appropriate avenues of distributing the resources of

the institution. The redirection of these resources away from "unnecessary" supervisory staff would be better spent, in Woodson's opinion, on the conservation and maintenance of local HBCU's.

Woodson's claim that the American African of his time had never received an education but instead had been informed "about other things he had not been permitted to do" (p. 144), sadly holds true today. One can easily step into an elementary school in 2012 and hold up two pictures, one of a famous hip hop artist like Lil' Wayne, and the other of famous pediatric surgeon Dr. Ben Carson, and observe the excitement exhibited in response to the photo of Lil' Wayne and the equally stunning blank stares in response to the picture of Dr. Carson. Similarly, you can ask American African medical school students about Imhotep. Many will not have a clue. But ask this same group about Hippocrates and they can make clear and detailed reference.

Ask any professor at the nation's HBCU's if special (equal) attention is given to the American African's contribution to the subject matter being studied. For example, in General Psychology courses, is sufficient time given to the contributions of American Africans such as S.O. Roberts or Francis Cecil Sumner to the discipline? Does one dare to examine and present African origins of many of the psychological concepts re-presented by Western Psychology? When studying Carl G. Jung, does the professor include Jung's studies in East African spiritual cultures, and his statements of the power and understanding he embraced because of these experiences? In this author's experience, it is rarely a part of this basic study, yet, whenever it is included and given equal respect, the students of African descent benefit greatly.

When this author has been invited to lecture at medical schools, the response is consistent from the American African student when information is presented about the African contributions to modern medical theory and practices as revealed by Dr. Charles Finch and others. The vibration of truth-speak resonates deep within the American African student and offers a bit of validation for their desire to be considered more than "mere" ex-slaves and minorities. Woodson's earlier notion that education is more than the imparting of information is strongly validated by such experiences. The author has received numerous notes from psychology students who have either enrolled in or simply attended one of his many courses on child development, abnormal psychology, or general psychology. These notes all have as a consistent theme the feeling of gratitude for introducing them to a method of teaching and subject matter that empowers and validates their (the student's) desire to become great in life.

This author is in agreement with the many suggestions offered in Woodson's new program, many of which are applicable today, with little to no modification. It is the author's feeling that the refinement suggested for the religious leaders who are maintaining the "old" way of teaching and handling their followers, should be equally applied to those who are educators; meaning, those educators who are unwilling or unable to update their beliefs, ideologies and methodologies to reflect a more progressive and truth supporting, culturally competent approach to the dissemination of information and the training of non-White professionals should also be "exiled." The direct and indirect teaching of non-White inferiority and the glamorization of European imperialism (including the pillaging of indigenous populations) should be a transgression tolerated by none. Unfortunately, it would take a more informed student population and perhaps a few more informed individuals in the ranks of the faculty to set and maintain a standard of disgust for such blatant ignorance being spewed in the halls of academia.

The pulpit pimping, religious manipulation and "holy rolling" should be equally intolerable. Regardless of one's religious affiliation and denomination, the masses would benefit from the true utilization of their religious precepts and examples as a standard against which to rate their leaders. If and when they are found to fall short, they should be treated as such, similar to how one would treat an individual with any other known issue. If one has demonstrated themselves to be a liar, then as a liar the wise person would approach them. If they have demonstrated themselves to be a manipulative thief, one should handle them accordingly. Likewise, if one has demonstrated themselves to be sincere, honest, and truly invested in the well being of their followers, they should receive treatment according to their works.

It seems that this level of common sense has been preached out of the masses using loosely interpreted points of scripture such as: "judge ye not lest ye be judged" or "let he who is without sin cast the first stone." The reality is that one could not survive without making judgments in their day to day, moment to moment lives. In fact, some would say that the quality of one's life is based on their ability to make consistently correct judgments and by acting according to their conclusions. As the author has traveled and lived amongst various cultures throughout the African diaspora, he has come across several groups of individuals who pray for and welcome judgment due to their feeling of living with clean hands and pure hearts. Clearly their perspective of judgment contradicts that taught by many modern churches.

The fear that many mis-educated American African's have around judging others is in part due to the fear that if they do so, they too will be judged. Why a person would fear judgment is most likely related to what they know of their own behavior, and how they believe they will be dealt with if those behaviors were to become publicly known. It's truly amazing that people would overlook the obvious consequences for their behaviors that have already occurred, and continue to conceal the acts as if this will somehow prevent the consequences from ever occurring.

A powerful remedy to this fear is found in a perspective shift. By simply highlighting the fact that they are being judged whether they are judging others or not, will serve to demystify the concept of judgment and empower the individual beyond the impossibility of living a life without judging. This point is important for the fact that American Africans and other oppressed populations have been slowly led into a state of docility and timidity in regards to their ability to hold others accountable based on their actions and/or inaction. Instead of being honest with themselves about their own misbehavior as well as that of their leaders, spouses, friends, etc., they tend to silently accept the sub-par behavior and/or treatment, and offer a wide range of excuses and self-blame for the situation.

The oppressed must at once throw off the shroud of mediocrity and begin to thrive and strive to improve in some aspect of life on a daily basis. There are plenty of self-concerns and issues given to each individual to keep him or her busy for the rest of their lives. The noble task of devoting one's self to the improvement of one's self is equal to none, and would perhaps exponentially decrease the oppressive burden experienced by this population. For example, if a person is aware of certain pending health challenges, based on genetic affiliation or lifestyle contributions, they could, under this "new, new program," begin to modify their habits to include those things that will strengthen their chances of preventing such issues from ever manifesting. On the flip side, they could modify their habits by taking away those risk factors that contribute to the likelihood of such potentialities becoming real.

Another major area of refinement under this "new, new program" is that of intimate relationships. Many of the burdens in the lives of individuals stem from the inability to initiate and maintain mature intimate relationships with another. Many in this day and time are chronic serial daters on a quest to find love. Ask this same group for a definition of love, and many, if not all, would struggle to define it in clear and concise terms. This lack of clarity demonstrates the futility of their "quest," however, it is not the fault of the confused. In fact, it is a clear testimony of how well the dumbing down process has worked.

We have been slowly and systematically trained to value and like ourselves less and less with each generation, beginning with the enslavement and subsequent forced breeding experienced by enslaved Africans. Over the generations, without any attempts to address and heal this highly traumatic and on-going experience, the American African has been confused and impoverished along the way. Today's hip hop generation is proof of the latent and transgenerational confusion that has existed within the American African family around the experience of enslavement and forced breeding. This point is evidenced by the ill regarded presentation of sexuality and the profane manner in which one expresses their sexual self.

This notion leads to another point proposed by the "new, new program." Parents, no matter how young or old, regardless of the number of children, it is strongly recommended that we all become more aware of the power to influence held and utilized by the media. One can simply observe the way a child watching television tends to "zone out." Verify this by calling a child's name at normal levels while they are zoned out (in trance) watching television. Most times, the child will not respond to the first two or three calls. You may have to change your tone or do something (i.e., physically tap them) to "wake" them up. Before waking them, pay special attention to the images, sounds, ideas, products, subtle images and messages that were actually holding them captive. Much of it is hidden in plain sight, others are consciously imperceptible to the observer unless they are able to pause, slow down, zoom in, or otherwise alter the presentation.

Corporations spend large amounts of money on their marketing strategies and often times pay a hefty sum to have their products or an image of their product "placed" in movies, videos, songs, behind home plate at baseball games, on the announcer's table at basketball games, or anywhere they can be easily, but subtly received by the unsuspecting observer. In hip hop music, it is the same. In this genre, rappers often weave products into their verse or chorus, seemingly not advertising. For example, rapper Talib Kweli on DJ Hi-Tek's sophomore album states "Manhattan was built on cemeteries where the Blacks was buried." This occurs in a song were fellow New York rapper Papoose states, "Pap grip the dessie [Desert Eagle gun] til that clip is empty. Man I'll have Black buried in the cemetery...you better tell holmes, messing with me will get Black buried like a cell phone." Whenever this song was played by the author in front of an audience who were subsequently asked to identify the product placement, invariably, no one was able to identify neither the product nor its placement. Once it is revealed, it becomes obvious. In many situations (possibly even this one) there is not an official agreement between artist, label, and company for the mention of their product...sometimes it just happens.

The author once asked a class of graduate psychology students to conduct a loose survey of undergraduate students to identify the most popular alcoholic beverage and where they first learned of the drink. The vast majority identified a particular brand of tequila and admitted to first hearing about it from a popular singer/rapper. In second place was a particular wine, which had also been featured in several pop culture songs and videos. This type of behavior modification is subtle yet highly effective. It literally has the potential to influence thoughts, speech, and/or actions of large populations, while the individuals believe they are generating their own independent and unique expressions.

Many students also admitted being introduced to the notion of getting high (smoking marijuana) initially by a relative, but finally began to partake as it was made popular and "cool" by hip hop artists. Today's hip hop references to drugs go beyond the mention of marijuana, often including prescription strength cough syrups containing codeine and promethazine, Rohypnol, MDMA (Ecstasy), lysergic acid diethylamide (lsd), and cocaine by their various names including: "drank," "roofies," "dipper," "molly," "pills," "powder," "white girl" "acid," "keisha," etc.

Products that are advertised are not only those which are purchasable at retail shops, but also include behaviors, attitudes and certain aspects of identity. For example, growing up, the author had an acquaintance that purchased a .380 handgun because his favorite rapper at the time had a song named after this particular pistol. He would literally walk around singing this song in reference to the concealed side-arm he was carrying...it became his weapon of choice to deal with adverse situations. Even the dances that people perform when certain songs come on at the club are dances that are often highlighted in music videos. When asked about their fashion-based desires, a large number looked to the hip hop artists to determine what was "hot" or acceptable at that time. Thoughts, beliefs, actions, attitudes, left up to these external sources, which may or may not have the child's best interest at heart, are potentially dangerous.

Once a parent or service provider becomes more aware, it would be most beneficial for them to begin monitoring and being far more selective regarding what their children are exposed too. This may require the adult in the home to alter their own media habits in the presence of children, which is a worthy sacrifice when one considers the potential to continue or break a cycle of confused patterns of behavior. Rather than allowing children to sit with the adults while they are watching television programs inappropriate for children (i.e., day and nighttime soap operas, violent programs, video countdown shows), the adult could find other times to watch the programs or otherwise occupy the child with more appropriate and creative activities. Should an adult choose to occupy the child with other activities while continuing to watch their own entertainment, the adult must take special care that the child is not vicariously partaking in the entertainment from a distance (still watching or listening to the television from the other room).

Children are able to gain valuable information from television watching, however, adults should be very selective of the programming. For example, children are easily fascinated by educational documentaries about nature, animals, cultures, etc. Although these too may contain subtle messages designed to persuade their perspective, they are less likely to have products placed and usually do not have commercials. They are also far more educational than most programs on commercial television.

Another point regarding the education and raising of children is the notion that reading is fundamental. Frederick Douglass once stated "reading and writing makes one unfit to be a slave." It is for this very reason that reading and writing were literally illegal for enslaved Africans. One can find numerous state laws that ascribed certain levels of punishment for those found attempting to read, write, or teach the same to the enslaved African. The power to read and write remains the same today. If a child is encouraged to read beginning at a young age, and if they are exposed to adults who read, they will be more likely to read when they get older. One very important factor in getting children to read is to allow them to read books that are interesting to them. Get a library card and use it. Regulate the number of hours spent on video games, television watching, and horseplay. Children must be prepared to be productive and would benefit most from having disciplined parents who value their child's future enough to do what is necessary now, to ensure them a chance later.

At first glance this may seem to be a little harsh. However, when one considers the large numbers of American African youth who are involved with the juvenile justice system, foster and adoptive services, substance use and abuse, psychiatric treatment programs, criminal behaviors, and without sufficient and mature parental influence, it becomes apparent that the larger part of an entire generation may be rendered ineffective right before our eyes. The reality of the situation, almost 80 years after Dr. Woodson shared his perspective on the mis-education of American Africans, is that the population may be in a worse position now than immediately following the abolishment of slavery. It is the illusion of freedom that makes the present situation so precarious. The notion that racism is a thing of the past and that the United States of America is now a "colorless" society based on the election of President Barack Obama is a fallacy that will cause a relaxing of one's analytical and defensive stance when it comes to the struggle for justice. It may also provide a false sense of security and accomplishment that invariably generates a premature celebration (much like the NFL player who began celebrating his "pending" touchdown prior to crossing into the end zone, only to have the ball knocked from his hands and the game lost).

Much of the monumental task identified and addressed by Dr. Woodson in 1933 remains a major burden for those interested in the restoration of the American African. In addition to the points laid out above by both Dr. Woodson and this author, the notion of a much-needed *Vocational Guidance* will now be explored.

Chapter 15

UJIMA: Collective Work and Responsibility
(Vocational Guidance)

"I am because we are; We are because I am."
-African Proverb

P ower, the ability to do work. Wasted power, a lack in the desire to do work, while being fully capable. One can choose any non-affluent, predominately American African community in the United States and drive through around 1pm on a warm day. They are almost guaranteed to find large numbers of able-bodied American African men and women standing around, some socializing, some loafing while others are hustling and participating in behaviors that directly result in incarceration. Widespread apathy and a low sense of self-efficacy seem to be the order of the day. Is it laziness? If so, why is it that so many American African youth are becoming this way, not wanting to put forth a reasonable effort towards the accomplishment of vital tasks? Some propose that it is inherent in the race. Others say it is a ploy by racism/White supremacy to maintain their control over the non-White population.

In a recent conversation with a real estate agent while searching for a home, the author pointed out the beautiful brick work of a property he was viewing. The agent was at once surprised that the potential client was paying such close attention to detail. The agent began to share information about how American African Brick Masons were systematically closed out of the market by union policies and overtly racist actions. He continued by explaining how he, being 25 years senior to the author, had observed the detrimental results of such actions on the morale and work ethic of those who were "locked out" of the industry. These Brick Masons initially fought to maintain their status as homebuilders and developers of buildings, however, many lost and began a downward spiral. The craft was no longer being passed down from one generation to the next as a viable means of earning a living; nor was it maintained as a noble and honorable skill by future generations. And thus, American Africans went from laying the bricks for the massive monuments and buildings in our nation's capital to hanging outside the "bricks" of our local housing projects.

The same goes for the American African Stone Masons of yesterday. They built many of the beautiful stonewalls and structures found throughout the U.S. They have figuratively gone from designing and building beautiful stone outback barbeque pits and houses to getting stoned while at barbeques. The contrast is sharp enough to cut diamonds. The industrious nature of the American African has been misdirected, thwarted, and all but snuffed out. Many young American Africans have no clue how their homes were built, and perhaps more importantly, how their food is produced. They are often astonished to find that they too can build structures to grow food right there at home.

In Woodson's day, the question of vocational guidance was answered by the advent of vocational programs for American Africans wherein they were taught trade skills in order to carry on as laborers. Although Woodson criticized the teaching of "skills" that were no longer appropriate and valuable in regards to being profitable or even practical, this author realizes that in the 21st century, these skills that were largely abandoned by American Africans would now serve to alleviate certain financial pressures associated with the high rates of under- and un- employment. For example, parents who choose to use cloth diapers for their newborn baby as opposed to store bought disposable diapers are capable of saving large amounts of money to be used in other areas of need. The same is true for a woman who learns how to create and maintain her own cloth "sanitary napkins" (maxi pads). Both males and females would do good to learn how to perform basic maintenance on their homes and cars and certain appliances around the house. These trades, while they may not be profitable in the sense of performing the tasks in order to generate money, are definitely beneficial for saving monies otherwise spent on these necessities.

Similarly families that maintain a garden at home are capable of producing certain food products enough to supplement certain meals or even generate entire meals for their household. Some are even able to take such a skill and generate a small family business known as a community supported agriculture (CSA) co-op, as did the Five Seeds Farm of the Baltimore area. Beyond the financial aspects of these trades, having and utilizing the aforementioned skills contributes greatly to the self-esteem and self-efficacy of the family. In fact, developmental theorist Erik Erikson juxtaposed the notion of industry against that of inferiority in his eight-stage theory of psychosocial development, noting how a child can either develop with an inferior disposition or an industrious one. This development is predicated in part by the child's ability to negotiate their environment and problem-solve, create opportunities and destroy obstacles for themselves.

Instead of capitalizing and making the necessary shifts in order to adopt these industrious practices, many carry on in a way that buries them deeper in the mold of despair and learned helplessness. Stated another way by Woodson:

> Most Negroes now employed are going down blind alleys, and unfortunately some schools seem to do no more than to stimulate their going in that direction...These facts have been known for generations, but some of these institutions apparently change not. Education, like religion, is conservative. Do not change the present order of thinking and doing, many say, for you disturb too many things long since regarded as ideal. The dead past, according to this view, must be the main factor in determining the future. We should learn from the living past, but let the dead past remain dead.
>
> (pp. 157-8)

Even today, education, like religion, remains conservative. Professors at HBCUs caution their students about using "too much Black stuff" in their presentations, papers, and perspectives. Students who offer scholarly rebuttals to the racist notions proffered by psychological theorists are labeled "rabble rousers" by their professors and dealt much retaliation for their "transgression." The student of African Studies is allowed to dabble in the political and social and even the cultural affairs of the African, but once they decide to incorporate some of the more practical and most important (foundational) aspects of those very societies (i.e., religious philosophies and spirituality) there arises a conflict with their current religious beliefs and the racist teachings ingrained therein. This internal conflict will surely be externalized; manifesting itself in the form of disappointed and disagreeing friends and family if one ever decides to take their quest deeper by attending an Ifa, Akan, Voudun, or Kemetic ritual in order to experience the culture of those whom they are studying.

Alternately, Europeans like John Mason, Placcid Temples, R.A. and Isha Schwaller de Lubicz, Carl G. Jung, and M.

Griaule & G. Dieterelen unapologetically submerge themselves into the spiritual cultures of the African in order to gain as full an understanding as possible. They then return from their experience and profit greatly from the information they are able to share as well as from the expanded perspective of reality gained while living amongst their respective populations of interest. We hold on to the "dead past," forsake "the living past," and wonder why we keep dying.

It is interesting how divided our scholars of yesterday were when trying to figure out how to improve upon the condition of the American African. The age-old argument was between those who felt that the American African was best served by an industrial-based education and those who advocated for the intellectual development of the race. In hindsight, the author is sure that all who participated in this futile debate would retract and begin to use those energies to develop a master plan to incorporate both perspectives in the total and holistic development of the American African. A similar argument that persists is that between the American African Christian, Muslim, Hebrew Israelite, Ifa devotee, Akan practitioner, etc. The power discoverable in the unification of the above named factions of an oppressed society would solve and eliminate a great deal of problems faced by American Africans; if only by retracting some of the energies wasted on the petty feuds about who is going to be "saved," who is an "infidel," who is "conscious," who is a "sell-out," etc., while in reality a large majority are presently living in "hell."

> Among people thus satisfied in the lower pursuits of life and sending their children to school to memorize theories which they never see applied, there can be no such thing as vocational guidance. Such an effort implies an objective…Opportunities which he has today may be taken from him tomorrow; and schools changing their curricula in hit-and-miss fashion may soon find themselves on the wrong track just as they have been for generations.

Negroes don't need some one to guide them to what persons of another race have developed. They must be taught to think and develop something for themselves. It is most pathetic to see Negroes begging others for a chance as we have been doing recently. 'Don't force us into starvation,' we said. 'Let us come into your stores and factories and do a part of what you are doing to profit by our trade.' The Negro as a slave developed this fatal sort of dependency; and, restricted mainly to menial service and drudgery during nominal freedom, he has not grown out of it. Now the Negro is facing the ordeal of either learning to do for himself or to die out gradually in the bread line in the ghetto. (pp. 159-60)

Some have felt that Dr. Woodson's statements in the above quote were a little extreme. However, 80 years later, there may actually be less collective efforts on the part of the American African, and far more dependency on others. For example, if the power (electricity) were to go out in any major U.S. city, how many American Africans would be prepared with alternative sources of energy? Sure there may be a supply of batteries for flashlights and a few candles to burn, but what about heat? Who knows how to build and sustain a fire for cooking or for keeping warm? Who owns supermarkets and are capable of ordering foods wholesale to redistribute at lower than market prices? Who in the community is skilled enough to build and repair shelters for living and protection? The knowledge and potential is there, en mass, however, the motivation and initiative needed to apply these skills is severely lacking.

More and more the younger populations are being psychologically and physically removed from the tangible natural environments. They are slowly becoming digitized and being reeled into the world of virtual reality. This is occurring through the medium of video games, internet sites, digital music streamed through digital components, "smart" cell phones, text messaging, chatting, and online universities. From one perspective, all of these technologies seem to mark advancement in civilization, yet, from another perspective, it is recognized as a clear regression in the form of social retardation.

As an educator, this author has witnessed first-hand how the over utilization of digital, non-verbal communication, can begin to deteriorate the existing verbal communication skills of an individual and a collective. Also hindered are the written communication skills of the individual. The first injury decreases the utilization of the spoken word to communicate ideas between two or more individuals. The majority of contact occurs through the medium of digital communication in the form of text messaging, "chatting" via instant messaging or a social networking site, and/or email (electronic mail). The second injury severely decreases an individual's ability to use the standard and accepted forms of written communication by altering the spelling and meaning of basic words and phrases (l8 = late, omg = oh my god, idk = I don't know).

These two injuries are detrimental to the viability and marketability of the individual. For example, if a person thus injured applies for a job that requires written and oral communication skills, they are unlikely to be able to pass the initial phases of the screening process. For it is unacceptable in most work environments to state in writing that: "I would prefer the l8 shift," as opposed to stating "I would prefer the late shift." This may seem to be an over exaggeration, however, the issue is actually being understated. The number of written communications that the author has received via email, as a college professor, where the entire message is written in lower case letters, without a greeting and without a closing to the message; or the number of times emails and assignments have been sent written in the language of a text message (n = in, ur = your, nsted = instead); or even the number of emails that are written entirely in the subject line is both astonishing and disheartening. It's almost as if the "smart phone" and other "smart" technology has dumbed down a generation; making it difficult to switch between forms and levels of communication carried out on the same device. A perhaps more profound effect of "smart" technology is the drastic decrease in verbal and non-technologically facilitated face-to-face communication (without the use of video phones, video conference, etc.).

The notion of collective work and responsibility, while intricately linked to the survival of any community, is also becoming more and more foreign and less and less likely to be a part of reality for those who remain totally "plugged in." It would greatly benefit any aspiring community to spend a great deal of time and resources towards the establishment of a system of accountability and responsibility for one's self and others within their sphere of influence. This notion, when coupled with the establishment of objectives designed to propel the group beyond mere survival mode into a mode of thriving, would begin to create a refined class of people who demand respect first from themselves, which will then be recognized and obliged by others.

This basic notion would begin to impact the detrimental experiences of the community's children almost immediately. For instance, if one objective was to decrease the exposure of children to second-hand cigarette smoke, then all adults would be vigilant about preventing others from smoking around their children. Adults who themselves smoke, would take whatever measures necessary to not expose children to their smoking, and/or to quit smoking altogether. This action alone would begin to curtail the high numbers of American African children being born with asthma and suffering from respiratory related ailments.

Another very simple and powerful action that can be immediately implemented and yield immediate and tangible results is that of increasing the number and level of family-based organized activities. This can take the form of family outings where several families meet at a local park to walk the trails together, or family dinner nights were several families come together to prepare and eat dinner together. This action can foster the building of lasting relationships between adults and their children. It also has the great potential of providing much needed financial support to those families who may be struggling or otherwise in need of assistance.

A major resource oft times overlooked are the skills and talents of those who live within one's community. Each individual is blessed with an ability that is easily converted into a valuable contribution to the collective. Many times, all that is needed is one who is capable of organizing these talents into a system that efficiently produces beneficial and practical results for the collective. This person is not the "leader" but instead, an individual who's talent is that of organizing, planning, and mobilizing people and resources.

Perhaps the most hindering factor to such progress is the lack of trust *and* trustworthiness of the oppressed. The lack of trust is fueled by countless experiences of betrayal, non-support, and opposition one gathers from the cradle to the grave. This notion of trust has deep implications and, according to some schools of thought, begins while developing in the womb. The notion of mistrust, in this context, begins for some when the mother is not nutritionally capable of sufficiently providing for the developing fetus. The fetus is then forced to begin extracting the resources from the mother's tissues (i.e., taking calcium and other minerals from the mother in order to grow itself which leads to tooth decay, pregnancy on-set diabetes, etc., in the mother). Stated differently, the fetus has to steal from its mother in order to survive. This is theorized to produce a sense of betrayal and a pessimistic view of the world, hence, an overall mistrust of the environment and those in it.

The notion of untrustworthiness is also linked to a lack of trust for others, and is thought to stem from the same roots. In a situation where one perceives resources to be scarce and where no one is capable of providing for their needs, individuals are more likely to resort to actions considered to be criminal and or harmful to society as a whole. This in turn leads to one being untrustworthy in the eyes of community and society. This lack of trust often simultaneously breeds jealousy, or vice versa. This jealousy, in turn, breeds a competitive attitude, which ultimately produces a need to duplicate and imitate the object of the negative emotion. It is theorized that at the core of jealousy is a strong desire to have an object or to be the person who has the object. As illustrated by Dr. Woodson:

> Such knowledge is especially necessary in the case of Negroes because of the fatal tendency toward imitation not only of the White man but the imitation of others in his own group. For example, a Negro starts a restaurant on a corner and does well. Another Negro, observing this prosperity, thinks he can do just as well by opening a similar establishment next door. The inevitable result is that by dividing the trade between himself and his forerunner he makes it impossible for either one to secure sufficient patronage to continue in business…(p. 167)

If instead of "parroting" the next person, individuals could assess for themselves the needs of those around them and somehow develop a method for meeting those needs that will also provide a sort of income for one's family, there wouldn't be a need for jealousy and petty bickering, back-biting, and the sabotaging of progress that is so prevalent amongst those found in oppressive situations. Mr. Dick Gregory once pointed out to the author that it is not the nature of the crabs in a pot to pull each other down, it's the boiling hot water that makes them act that way. This analogy is totally applicable to the current situation experienced daily by American Africans around the world. To extinguish the fire boiling the water in the pot and/or tipping the pot must become the collective top priority for both those already in the pot and for those likely to be placed therein.

In order for this to be done, more American Africans must be trained in the behavioral sciences as competent practitioners who are not only capable of applying the learned techniques as prescribed, but also capable of applying them in a culturally competent and efficient manner to those whom they are deciding to treat and eventually cure. This training will assist in understanding the true nature of the crab (American African), the programmed and/or reactionary actions of the crab (American African), and the scientific methods for preventing and/or reversing the resulting behaviors when one is exposed to stimuli/pressure (boiling water) designed to cause detrimental behaviors in the population.

This is more than a notion. This requires one to carry on a dualistic sort of education; one that includes the typical and standard training provided in the programs of choice, as well as a training in culture that goes beyond an intellectual treatment of the "way of life" of the people in question; one that affords a deep level of understanding of the belief systems and world views of the population (including spiritual, religious, etc.). This training is vital in order to correct the lack of understanding currently consuming the lives of American Africans. It will provide that beacon of light necessary for addressing those psycho-spiritual issues that come as a natural result of the treatment (past and present) of a violently oppressive and manipulative society. Hence, we urgently need the development of a *New Type of Professional*," one that is capable of going above and beyond the individualistic "American Dream" of securing a house, car, spouse and children, but one who aspires for the larger "American Dream," that is, one who is employed for the purpose of establishing justice for the sake of life, liberty, and the pursuit of happiness.

Chapter 16

Universal Man and Universal Woman
(A New Type of Professional Man Required)

*"A Universal Man and/or Universal Woman is any male, and/
or any female, person, who knows and understands truth, and,
who has used that knowledge and understanding in a manner
that has produced justice and correctness, in all places,
in all areas of activity, including Economics, Education,
Entertainment, Labor, Law, Politics, Religion, Sex, and War."*
**-Mr. Neely Fuller, Jr.
The United-Independent Code/System/Concept for
Thought, Speech, and/or Action. A Textbook/Workbook for
Victims of Racism (White supremacy)**

*"The world is not circumscribed by the United States, and the
Negro must become a pioneer in making use of a larger portion
of the universe."*
**Carter G. Woodson
The Mis-Education of the Negro**

The continued attempts to solve the problems of oppressed
populations solely through the use of tools, processes and
procedures provided by the oppressor is to continually waste
time, resources and energy. Unfortunately, this is what many
American Africans are doing by the thousands, every day,
in some of our most resourceful institutions, including our
colleges and universities. We are continually producing more

and more well-trained, but ill-prepared American Africans who are intelligent, degreed, yet have never passed the test of "orientation" as one would during a mental status exam, prior to being declared competent enough to go about their daily lives unimpeded.

This orientation involves the ability of a person to identify who they are, where they are, and when the present moment exists in space and time. More plainly, a competent person is capable of stating their name/identity, where they are presently located (city, state, exact building location), and usually the date (month, day and year) of the present moment. These three variables are utilized to identify one's competence because the confusion about any one of these variables can serve to disorient an individual, and thus render them less effective in their daily activities.

In the case of the American African professional, this very orientation is what tends to be absent from their professional development. Throughout the average American African's educational career, one is rarely exposed to a sustained experience wherein they are given truthful and empowering information about who, what, where, when and why they are in life. They will rarely be given a true education about their status as a victim of racism/White supremacy.

Very seldom is one presented with information regarding one's heritage and ancestry extending beyond the plantation and colonial experience of their more recently passed generations. And rarely is a truthful perspective presented to the American African regarding their political and social relationship with the ruling and oppressive class of individuals. Instead, they tend to be purposely disoriented to believe that their history and experience with civilization begins with the enslavement and colonization of their ancestors by European colonizers, pirates and raiders; and that the then system of racism and White supremacy is totally separate and distinct from the current system of racism and White supremacy, which maintains the structure of society and governs international, political and economical interactions amongst non-White and White nations.

Business majors and business women and men are not taught the history of the stock market and how certain corporations/institutions got their financial starts, directly or indirectly, from the colonization and or enslavement of African peoples and nations. This bit of information, if known, is rarely tied into the current economic disparities between White and non-White businesses. It is rarely highlighted that the great disparities between the first and third world nations of the world are largely based on this conquest. The contradiction is apparent if one is given the proper lens through which to observe the phenomenon. For example, many nations labeled "undeveloped" and "underdeveloped" or even "developing" are the same nations that supply a vast amount of resources for the "developed" and "first world" nations. Some may argue that it is the underdeveloped aspects of the nation that keeps the government from monetizing its natural resources for its own benefit and profit. In a case such as this, the author would gently guide the arguer to a study in colonialism and its frequent and rapid extraction of the raw materials from resource rich nations such as the Congo, and how the great rubber companies have "repaid" the people and government of the Congo.

Additionally, educators are taught the history of education in the United States excluding the numerous state laws that made it illegal for enslaved Africans, and even those who were recently "freed," to teach and/or learn how to read and write. If they are privileged enough to get this information, it is not shared in a way that makes it easy to identify the relationship between such an historical atrocity and the current low-achievement and academic performance of American Africans. Medical doctors are often given their medical information, standards, biological norms, etc., as they have been standardized on White populations, despite the wealth of information demonstrating the different norms for various cultural and racial groups. Neither are these professionals provided with sufficient information concerning the environmental and social impact of racism on health outcomes of non-White peoples. Child psychologists and early childhood educators are not taught the various behavioral norms and outcomes of non-White children as compared to those of White children. They are not given a complete analysis of Mary Ainsworth's *Infancy in Uganda* regarding the differing developmental milestones of African descendants and how this translates into educational pedagogy, learning and teaching methods.

The above are just a few of the ongoing list of examples demonstrating how information may be handled to orient or disorient a group of people including those entrusted to be the healers, educators and fashioners of society. The knowledge of these educationally-based issues should serve as a call for the refinement of the present systems of professional preparation. This refinement should include the adoption of a parallel process that simultaneously develops a well informed, and culturally conscious, effective, and competent individual who understands the scope and impact of racism and White supremacy on the daily lives of White and non-White people globally.

This new group of professionals must be critical in their thinking regarding all things that impact people, in all areas of human activity including: Economics, Education,

Entertainment, Labor, Law, Politics, Religion, Sex, and War/ Counter War. This does not mean that one must become an angry, "militant," paranoid person who hates all things white (including toilet paper, animals, clouds, etc.). However, this does mean that a new breed of professionals will stand for justice, on behalf of non-White people, without apology and without the self-censoring fear that causes some to buckle at the thought of offending the established system of injustice.

The new professional must be learned and well-read in all matters concerning human experience and beingness. If one is a carpenter, they should be capable of interacting, intellectually and/or practically, with certain aspects of the healing arts, just as a dentist should have some degree of understanding civil, corporate and various aspects of the law. An educator should also exercise certain practical skills as a plumber, electrician, HVAC technician or any other trade that will allow them to develop and hone a variety of mental abilities and physically dependent skills. Perhaps more importantly, education should involve a concise process of spiritual cultivation designed to increase consciousness, physical health, cognitive functioning, and foster the development of a healthy and progressive identity.

The notion of a healthy and progressive identity is based on the premise that one's identity basically defines their perspective of their own capabilities, locus of control, purpose in life, and sense of self-worth. It is unfortunate but true that a large number of American Africans are self-identifying as "niggers" and are simultaneously being shown how others who also self-identify as the same are "rewarded" with money, power, fame, and respect. The term "rewarded" is used here in the context of operant conditioning for the purpose of demonstrating how the identity of a "nigger" is defined, broadcast far and wide through print, video, and music, and then rewarded (record deals, keys to the city, high budget video shoots, concerts, money, fame, etc.); all of which increases the likelihood that these behaviors will be imitated and continued.

The reality is that many of these self-identified "niggers" are paid actors, playing a part and following the script. This was probably truer at the beginning of hip hop than it is now due to the fact that close to 30 years have passed since NWA (Niggaz With Attitudes) and other self-proclaimed "niggers" first introduced this wave of dehumanization to American Africans via this medium. During this span of time, American Africans have had the opportunity to internalize the message and behavior patterns of "niggers," give birth to their own children, whom are also "affectionately" referred to as "my little nigga" while simultaneously being exposed to ever more sophisticated doses of the "nigger" image. It is from this pool that some of the newer hip hop artists are being selected; "real gangsters" who have tasted the hardship of racism, poverty, violence and neglect.

The desire to become a superstar "nigger" is far more popular than the desire to cultivate one's identity to the level of a "conscious" and "liberated" being. This phenomenon is often clouded when certain of these self-proclaimed "niggers" receive the title of being "conscious" and progressive. The confusion occurs because statements such as this are often taken as the "gospel truth" and rarely examined (see Lupe Fiasco's "Bitch Bad" video).

For example, Tupac Shakur, having a strong connection with the Black Panthers via his mother Sister Afeni Shakur, step-father Dr. Mutulu Shakur, and God-father Geronimo Pratt, was often considered to be a conscious or revolutionary rapper. He coined the phrases T.H.U.G. L.I.F.E. (The Hate You Give Little Infants Fucks Everybody) and N.I.G.G.A.

(Never Ignorant Getting Goals Accomplished), and even formulated the "Code of the Thug Life" with Dr. Mutulu Shakur as a means to regulate the escalating gang violence amongst American Africans and Spanish speaking youth. These accomplishments coupled with his fame and ability to relate to younger generations has led to people waving the 2Pac banner, celebrating the "thug life" and his music.

Many of these people are well-respected scholars and otherwise notable persons in society who seemingly do not represent what is overtly expressed in the majority of 2Pac's music. For example, I couldn't imagine Dr. Michael Eric Dyson in his autobiography stating: "I won't deny it, I'm a straight rider. You don't wanna fuck with me…" Or my dear sister Nikki Giovanni exclaiming "M.O.B. (money over bitches)" when asked how she prioritizes her time.

The author is a 2Pac fan and has all of his pre-death albums (including his Don Killuminati release under the pseudonym of Makavelli). The author knows the lyrics to almost every song on each of these albums and can even flow in "real-time" with Pac. This author also knows the impact of being devoted to this musical message, and what it can do to a young and developing mind. For example, the author was once a self-proclaimed "nigger" who walked, talked, and behaved as we are instructed by the more famous, rewarded and accomplished "niggers."

The author has also experienced first hand how 2Pac's "image" has impacted certain individuals in the diaspora, specifically in The Gambia, West Africa. While there on a study abroad trip, the author was approached by a teenaged Gambian brother while walking down the road in the coastal town of Bakau. The Gambian excitedly approached the author holding his necklace and pointing to the gun-shaped charm hanging from it. While gesturing towards the pistol on his necklace, the young man exclaimed "What's up my nigger? What's up my nigger? I'm 2Pac, I'm 2Pac." His ancestors were truly turning in their graves.

Surely this was an isolated incident and is no way indicative of a wider trend regarding 2Pac's image and impact in Africa, right? Almost a decade later, the author was researching and watching the documentary *Bling*. This informative and powerful video delves deeply into the "blood diamond" phenomenon of Sierre Leone through the eyes of several hip hop and reggaeton artists. There is a deep and astonishing revelation that occurs when the African "street soldiers" are highlighted and shown wearing their "uniforms" of 2Pac t-shirts as they pillage and rampage villages.

The point of the above discourse regarding the propagation of self proclaimed "niggers" is to point out a very powerful and thriving source of influence that has taken precedence in the American African culture. Nonetheless, challenging the bad "rap" that hip hop is getting, Jay Z (Shawn Carter) states: "Scarface the movie, did more than Scarface the rapper to me…" While this may be true, Scarface the rapper (Brad Jordan) states: "…while listening to Brad [Scarface the rapper], David gets pissed and kills his dad." Each rapper's statement serving to illustrate how, in some form or another, media is capable of influencing the decision making processes of the impressionable consumer.

As discussed by Mr. Neely Fuller, Jr., the area of people activity known as "entertainment" serves as a powerful tool for both oppression and liberation. It's clear that it is not widely used for the latter (liberation), and that many are totally oblivious to its use as a tool for the former (oppression). Hence, the need for a system of education designed to increase consciousness and one that fosters a sense of a progressive and healthy identity. According to Fuller, this type of training would culminate in the production of what he refers to as Universal Men and Universal Women.

To perceive oneself as a Universal Man or a Universal Woman, means that one has no predefined place or limitation in life, but instead, has free range and access to the universe as a whole. At first glance, this seems to be a very esoteric and philosophical concept, however, after further investigation, it proves itself to be a more realistic and beneficial perspective for an individual in an oppressed situation to adopt. This perspective will do more than boost self-esteem, but will also systematically deconstruct externally and erroneously imposed false limitations on the mind, body and spirit of those who have been deceitfully bound by the oppressive desires of another.

This notion follows closely the subtle teachings of the first three degrees of Freemasonry, wherein the candidate undergoes gradual intellectual training in the physical, mental, and spiritual aspects of his being. Just like in the lodge of the Entered Apprentice, Fellow Craft, and Master Mason, this information regarding the universality of one's potential must be further explored "outside of the Lodge" and practiced in day-to-day life in order for the depths of the teachings to be further revealed and made habitual to one's understanding, thinking, and doing. Similar to the results of a well constructed process taking place in the Blue Lodge, a person who endeavors to become Universal will likewise be "raised from the dead" in order to be born again in a new Light. Meaning their perspective of self, others, nature and the creator will undoubtedly become empowered, as will their ability to change their circumstances.

This revolutionary thought is not new, nor is it limited to the salvation of American Africans. In fact, if one were to study the indigenous cultures of the world, one would find that before Ancient Africans claimed to be Africentric (African-centered) they were oriented by the natural movements of the universe, and derived their daily customs from this knowledge and experience. Archaeologists are currently supporting the notion that the most stable civilizations and structures ever known to the planet are those which were and are constructed based on these universal principles. Physicists are now studying patterns in nature that provide seemingly illogical, yet virtually impenetrable structures, that are duplicated on both the micro and macro levels. These structures are based on universal patterns occurring naturally with no input from human intellect. An astonishing example is how a beehive is naturally antibacterial, antiviral and antifungal; and how each cell in a beehive is constructed in a perfect geometric formation, which is necessary for the nurturance and development of the future generation of bees.

Observing and challenging aspects of our own lives that have been limited by both internal conditionings and externally imposed boundaries, reveals how easily many false notions and beliefs are disproven and discarded. These limitations will undoubtedly yield to the exertion of one's reclaimed identity, which is based on a more thorough understanding and knowledge of what it is to be a human being. A perfect example of this concept is found in the popular movie *The Truman Show* starring Jim Carrey. In this movie, the main character, Truman, is an unknowing participant in a "reality show" about his "life." He does not realize that every aspect of his life has been scripted and that he is actually living on a movie set. The creators, directors and producers of Truman's contrived life control everything from the rising of the sun (really a high powered-mobile lamp suspended in the studio's ceiling) to the "implantation" of certain traumatic experiences to create phobias in his mind. Similar to *The Matrix*, there is a person who has been awakened who then strives to awaken "Truman" to the false world in which he has been enslaved.

Everyone in this film knew the inherent value of "Truman." His fan base was tremendous, with millions of people having followed him from his days in the womb, up to his final bow. For the vast majority of his life, he never realized how much people benefitted from his ignorance; and how well orchestrated his state of confusion had been. He could never have imagined that *everything* in his world, including his personality, identity, family, perspective, fears, thoughts, speech and actions, were all products of those who intended to maintain his oppression. Once he became even slightly aware of this situation, he grew in courage and defiance until at last, he liberated himself.

What will it take for you to do the same? From whence will the courage of the masses come? What will motivate those who are struggling towards "*Higher Strivings…*?"

Chapter 17

Higher Strivings in the Service of Yourself
(Higher Strivings in the Service of the Country)

"If the oppressor won't treat you right, what makes you think he will teach you right?"
-Khalid Abdul Muhammed

In 1899, as a part of his phenomenal study *The Philadelphia Negro*, W. E. B. Du Bois published the following five points and duties that must be assimilated and carried out by those living within the jurisdiction of the post-Civil War United States, if there was ever to be peace and justice in this nation:

1) The Negro is here to stay.
2) It is to the advantage of all, both Black and White, that every Negro should make the best of himself.
3) It is the duty of the Negro to raise himself by every effort to the standards of modern civilization and not to lower those standards in any degree.
4) It is the duty of the White people to guard their civilization against debauchment by themselves or others; but in order to do this it is not necessary to hinder and retard the efforts of an earnest people to rise, simply because they lack faith in the ability of that people.
5) With these duties in mind and with a spirit of self-help, mutual aid and cooperation, the two races should strive side by side to realize the ideals of the republic and

make this truly a land of equal opportunity for all men.

These statements were issued as a "bottom-line," "straight, no chaser" proposition regarding the future of race relations and the equal distribution of responsibility for the establishment of justice in America. His first point regarding the permanent presence of "the Negro" has much to do with the perceived attempts to "wish" American Africans into oblivion (accompanied by many instances of brutal violence, murder, kidnapping, lynching, etc.). Thirty-six years after the emancipation of enslaved Africans, the nation was still in deep turmoil, unrest, and chaos, while trying to simultaneously rebuild and control large numbers of "displaced" plantation prisoners. During this time, many Whites wanted to rid "their" country as well as their consciousness of the ever-present stigma associated with their peculiar institution, slavery.

Du Bois' statement was a sort of reality check for those who fantasized about a world without the American African in both the former enslaved state as well as the inevitably healed and empowered state. It was also a psychological ploy used to quell or decrease the instances in which White Americans acted out this latent desire to rid the nation of American Africans. On an unconscious level, the "anxiety" associated with the American African presence may have stemmed from what many have called "the reckoning"; that is, the moment or period of time in which the re-emerging African would possibly decide to seek restitution and perhaps visit the same levels of violence upon their former enslavers that had been visited upon them as slave, which leads to Du Bois' 2nd point.

Indeed, it would greatly benefit all parties involved to see that the newly emancipated African receives every available opportunity to be restored and to restore themselves to the level of fully functioning human beings with a healthy and adaptive culture intact. This would begin to level the playing field and empower the emancipated African with tools to rebuild levels of consciousness that are necessary for healing the trans-generational traumas associated with enslavement.

Point number three specifically addresses American Africans as the source of their own development and reparations. With a sympathetic heart, Du Bois acknowledges the need for the newly emancipated African to "catch up" to current technologies and standards of "civilization"; he emphasizes the notion that the standards must be held firm in spite of the existence of rampant injustice. In essence, this point was an attempt to return the locus of control back to the emancipated African, and out of the hands of the former enslaver. This monumental task is and was easier said than done. It would require a refinement of the conditioned psychology maintained by the emancipated African and those Whites accustomed to being dominant and superior.

Logically the next point addresses the perspective of those Whites who, by force of habit and continued confusion, maintain the thoughts, speech and/or actions of the White supremacist culture. These Whites are put on notice that if indeed you are only attempting to protect your civilization and its principles, it is not necessary to injure and prevent another from contributing to the same. In other words, Du Bois was pointing out the hypocrisy of those who boasted of defending "old glory" and the papered ideas of the Founding Fathers while simultaneously being the source of the very debauchment they were fighting against. Du Bois recognized that some of the White Americans were oblivious to this hypocrisy while others were not only aware, but were intentionally so.

His fifth and final point is an appeal to the moral and conscientious aspect of being human. Keeping with the theme of self-determination and unity, coupled with an assumption that the four previous points are agreed upon by all parties, Du Bois sets forth the marching orders for establishing and maintaining justice in the United States of America. He advocates for individuals of all races and cultures to run parallel courses towards the goal of realizing the vision of the Founding Fathers, that is, to make America "the land of the Free, and the home of the Brave." Many have experienced the contrary and know all too well that it will take an immense amount of bravery to establish and maintain freedom.

How do these five points offered by W.E.B. Du Bois relate to what Dr. Woodson proffers in terms of *higher strivings*? As demonstrated by the following quote, Woodson also saw the quest towards justice as a function of self-determination, unification, and the development of individuals into their optimal state, in order that they may function beyond reproach.

> Another factor the Negro needs is a new figure in politics, one who will not concern himself so much with what others can do for him as with what he can do for himself. He will know sufficient about the system of government not to carry his trouble to the federal functionaries and thus confess himself a failure in the community in which he lives. He will know that his freedom from peonage and lynching will be determined by the extent that he can develop into a worthy citizen and impress himself upon his community. (p. 181)

It is important to understand that Woodson's use of the word "politics" is consistent with the modern and popular use of the word which often refers to the realm of elected officials and their process of executing, adjudicating, and legislating on behalf of, and sometimes in spite of, the non-elected citizen. Although the above definition is functional, the author would like to continue this discussion using the following definition of politics as offered by Mr. Neely Fuller, Jr.:

"Any interaction between two or more people in any area of people activity

including: Economics, Education, Entertainment, Labor, Law, Politics, Religion, Sex, and War/Counter-War."

From this perspective, Du Bois' and Woodson's notions of becoming a more capable and fully functioning individual, in order to enhance the growth and development of this nation, becomes more credible as a means for actually achieving this goal. With people interactions as the focus, one begins to see how important and essential individual self-development and education are to the outcomes of groups and entire nations; and how important it is for each and every citizen to become an outstanding "politician," fully capable of advocating for their own needs and rights to live as a sovereign being; free from the imposed and biased perspectives of those who advocate for injustice in their daily thoughts, speech and/or actions.

To check debauchery within one's own group, as stated by Du Bois, would first require an open and honest assessment of the group, its historical patterns of behavior, its current attitudes and beliefs concerning justice, as well as the full accounting of instances where injustice has been manifested by individuals comprising that group. This task is major and would be considered arduous by many, nonetheless, if true justice is to be established and maintained, it must be undertaken. Such an endeavor would serve to separate the "chaff from the wheat," in order that betrayers of the "justice movement" may be readily identified and engaged accordingly.

Furthermore, unification of goals must also become a reality. For example, if the improvement of education is agreed to be a worthy cause, all those with a vested interest in the education of people should agree to make this their joint priority, and agree to take the most efficient and effective paths toward these goals. It is important to emphasize that each group and or individual may indeed operate more effectively than another along a specific and unique path; this is to be honored and should never become a divisive factor. If one group feels the Montessori approach is most beneficial to the growth and development of their children, by no means should this be obstructed, if in fact it is demonstrated to be without harm; if another group feels that culturally-centered, race-based education is most valuable, then by all means, this group should maximize and perfect this opportunity to bring about justice as regards the education of their children. Again, as long as the common goal of establishing justice in this nation is adhered too, then there should be no injustice born through the processes.

As illustrated in an earlier chapter, it is far too common for small groups of people to become further diminished in number and become less politically effective through the over-emphasizing of religious differences. In becoming a more efficient and effective citizen, the individual will have to strive to understand the point at which all religious beliefs converge and form a tangent with one another. If this is impossible, it becomes necessary that the individual learn to accept the differences between the religions just as they would accept the difference between their heart and their lungs, understanding that both are essential when a common goal is shared, even if the mechanics behind their operation is not fully understood.

This refined level of politics (people interaction) would surely minimize the occurrence of conflict and non-productive engagements. This refinement would indeed raise the standards across the board. No longer will American Africans accept the label and identity of "nigger," but will instead reject all instances of its presence, just as Whites will reject all instances of racism from within their race, making it equally unacceptable and intolerable.

The new, self-assured, clear and focused citizen, will gain from becoming as mentally and physically healthy as possible; optimizing their knowledge and behaviors regarding their personal well-being. If, for example, it is known that illicit drugs carry not only a legal, but also a health burden, the new citizen will dismiss all temptations and notions supporting the use, distribution and manufacturing of these substances. If particular dietary habits have been identified as having detrimental effects on the overall well-being of the individual, then these habits will also be rejected and replaced with those that are more beneficial and constructive to the individual and group as a whole.

Ignorance and reactionary politics will no longer hold an esteemed place amongst the new citizen. It too will be rejected and refined into a more effective and efficient state of knowledgeable and contemplative interactions. No longer will the notion of "being smart" be considered "acting White" by the non-White people of the world, but each will instead understand their own racial group's contribution to the legacy of human growth in knowledge and understanding. This empowering stance against ignorance will serve the nation well. Once again everyday people will be amongst inventors and paradigm shifters, who apply their mental energies towards the improvement of society and the planet as a whole.

> Why wait for a spur to action when he finds his manhood insulted, his women outraged, and his fellowmen lynched for amusement? The Negroes have always had sufficient reason for being radical, and it looks silly to see them taking up the cause of others who pretend that they are interested in the Negro when they merely mean to use the race as a means to an end. When the desired purpose of these so-called friendly groups will have been served, they will have no further use for the Negro and will drop him... (p. 188)

So what is it that keeps the American African and other races from standing up and championing the cause of justice? Why are people more interested in global and often intangible causes than those that are local and carry a personal element? Why is it that so many American Africans have no clue about their present situation, how it came to be, how it differs from their former role on the planet, and how it can be restored to a place of humanity and dignity? Is it perhaps because relatively few American Africans have taken on the task of studying their own legacy beyond the plantation and European colonialism? Could it be due to the lack of emphasis on the pre-Modern era of history that many feel there is no African presence in the world prior to enslavement? Let us explore the rewards that exist in *The Study of the Negro* as outlined in Woodson's final chapter.

Chapter 18

Self Knowledge: The Key to All Knowledge
(The Study of the Negro)

"Man Know Thy Self in Order to Know God..."
Ancient Egyptian Proverb

"It is unfortunate that so much of the history of Africa has been written by conquerors, foreigners, missionaries and adventures. The Egyptians left the best record of their history written by local writers. It was not until near the end of the 19th century when a few European scholars learned to decipher their writing that this was understood."
Why Africana History
John Henrik Clarke

In an article entitled "Why Africana History," Dr. Clarke expounds on the numerous reasons why he and others like George G.M. James, Anna Julia Cooper, John Jackson, Dorothy Burnett Porter Wesley, Yosef ben Jochannan, Marion Thompson Wright, Ivan Van Sertima, Drusilla Dunjee Houston, Leonard Jeffries, Zora Neale Hurston, Elsie Lewis, Maulana Karenga, Merze Tate, J.A. Rogers, Helen G. Edmonds, Cheik Anta Diop, Frances Ellen Harper Watkins, John Hope Franklin and Pauline E. Hopkins, sacrificed and risked their lives to research the truth regarding the African contribution to the world, both past and present.

Dr. Clarke, in defense of his perspective, states the following facts plain and simple:

> Africa and its people are the most written about and the least understood of all of the world's people. This condition started in the 15th and the 16th centuries with the beginning of the slave trade and the colonialism system. The Europeans not only colonized most of the world, they began to colonize information about the world and its people. In order to do this, they had to forget, or pretend to forget, all they had previously known about the Africans. They were not meeting them for the first time; there had been another meeting during Greek and Roman times. At that time they complemented each other.

The implications of such an action (specifically the enslavement and colonization of the world and information about the world) are readily observable in modern times. The historical record has been so greatly skewed that criminals have been made to appear heroic, and victims seem to be the aggressor. Founders of great civilizing knowledge, information and cultures have been "hypothesized" to be alien visitors, while rapists and pillagers have been labeled explorers and "God-ordained" founders of great societies.

A deeper aspect of the colonization of information is the colonization of the mind, along with identity, self-concept, one's value system, and even an individual's and their community's sense of efficacy. This is why, as Woodson states, "the large majority of Negroes have become interested in the history and status of other races, and they spend millions annually to promote such knowledge." He continues, "Along with this sum, of course, should be considered the large amount paid for devices in trying not to be Negroes." (p. 190)

To render a group invisible, unimportant, subhuman, and without merit is to cripple their potential for future success and accomplishments, while simultaneously setting the stage for their disregard and disrespect. This has set up the "self-checked" condition that is experienced by large numbers of American Africans and is exactly what Woodson referred to in the following statement:

> The oppressor...teaches the Negro that his race has done nothing significant since the beginning of time, and that there is no evidence that he will ever achieve anything great. The education of the Negro then must be carefully directed lest the race may waste time trying to do the impossible. Lead the Negro to believe this and thus control his thinking. If you can thereby determine what he will think, you will not need to worry about what he will do. You will not have to tell him to go to the back door. He will go without being told; and if there is no back door he will have one cut for his special benefit. (p. 192)

How does this look in 2012? Let's start by referring back to the self-identification of many American Africans as niggers (niggaz, niggas, etc.). This is more than just a label (see next chapter). This once "racial slur" used by enslavers of Africans to degrade and further demean a once noble people, has grown into a complex personality construct, complete with identifying traits and characteristics. The majority of these traits are consistently negative, and open the way for less than beneficial consequences to be experienced by its bearer.

For example, many individuals in the media who self-identify as niggers (niggaz, niggas, etc.), specifically rappers/hip hop artists, tend to also promote criminal and violent behaviors as a core aspect of their identity. Outside of the studio or video shoot, these behaviors would likely get an individual arrested, incarcerated, and maybe even murdered. The issue arises when these actors (for those who are acting) are influencing the larger population of American Africans to imitate these behaviors in the "real world," where they then experience the "real world" consequences.

In a sense, this subtle influence is marketing a particular set of behaviors in order to increase the participation in certain industries (i.e., prisons, mortuary services, hospitals, the streets, etc.). At its core, all marketing is but a behavior modification tool, used to get people to start doing something they haven't done (smoking cigarettes), continue doing something they already do (continue smoking cigarettes despite the negative health experiences), or change the way they are doing what they currently do (switch brands of cigarettes).

One need but observe the ever growing numbers of youth, uneducated, mis-educated, and "educated" that refer to themselves as niggers (niggaz, niggas, etc.) on a regular and consistent basis; who answer when called nigger (nigga, etc.) by their friends, family and associates. Pay special attention to the attitude, the values, the priorities, the goals and visions maintained by this group. Across the board, the majority want to be, in some way, like those famous self-proclaimed niggers (niggaz, niggas, etc.) who popularized and modeled the role. From the elementary schools to the HBCU you will find that those who self-identify as niggers (niggaz, niggas, etc.) also tend to participate in a large amount of self-defeating/self-destructive behaviors; and share the same level of vision or lack thereof.

The number of fathers who refer to their sons as "my little nigga," the number of females who refer to their male counterparts as "my nigga," and the number of friends who refer to their friends as "my nigga" is alarming, yet it is in such a high number that it has indeed become the "norm." The ordinary response to such a dialogue as this (one that breaches this sensitive topic) is to become defensive and to attack the one offering such a controversial perspective; nonetheless, this author is not discouraged nor deterred by that potential. In fact, the author writes from experience, as an individual who once believed himself to be a "nigger" (nigga); and who once carried himself in such a way that he fit the personality profile ascribed to "niggers" (niggaz, niggas).

Once, while conducting a training on mental health and identity at a prestigious southern medical school, the author raised his concerns about people self-identifying as "niggers" (niggas, niggaz). He continued by showing how the behaviors modeled by famous and influential "niggers" (niggaz, niggas) are those that are harmful, self-destructive, and at times detrimental to those with whom they interact. Afterwards a White lady who identified herself as a recovering crack addict thanked the author for such an interesting and compelling presentation. She excitedly described how she is usually very inattentive during presentations but that she was somehow captivated by the author's discussion on the mind and identity. She continued by sharing how she always uses the word "nigger" because she is "in the streets" and that's how "we" talk to each other. She then verbalized her newly found awareness that "it does carry some behaviors that just ain't right…and people do act a certain way when we see ourselves as niggers…"

The author was more than grateful for her honesty and genuinely communicated that to her. She did not censor herself because her use of the word, even as a White female, was not to offend, nor was it to degrade. What she realized during this presentation is that the term is used amongst those who have already been socially degraded and outcasted. In a room with well over 200 people, 75% of which were American Africans, she was, surprisingly, the only one to respond directly to my statements of the "nigger" (nigga) identity.

The creation of a special "backdoor" tends to take the form of illicit substance use, risky behaviors, social irresponsibility, and the lack of motivation in regards to personal health and well-being. The author agrees that many of the aforementioned examples are learned behaviors that may or may not have been intentionally taught to the American African as a continuation of enslavement. The author also realizes that presently, there is a high level of cultural reinforcement that helps these negative behaviors and attitudes to continue amongst a certain group of people. Nonetheless, it is for those of us who know better to do better and eventually to teach others to do the same.

This opportunity for self-assessment is one that should not be taken lightly. It can be the first domino touched, setting off a chain reaction to topple the plethora of negative statistics accounting for the American African's condition. If, for example, students enrolled in psychology programs were taught about operant conditioning using culturally relevant examples of how people are influenced into everyday self-destructive behaviors through the system of rewards, punishment, positive and negative reinforcements, as well as through classical conditioning, they would be more aware of the context in which they live. If children were raised with a better understanding of the human body as an amazing and divinely-created vehicle, how it functions, how it is healed and harmed, they would be more likely to take care of, enhance and protect it.

If starting from a young age, children in modern societies were taught their positive value and expected contributions to their community, along with their purpose in life, they would be more likely to grow into productive and powerful citizens. If parents were encouraged to enhance their own understanding of human development prior to becoming parents, and definitely after conception, our societies stand a better chance of having well-adapted, healthy, and minimally traumatized individuals within them.

If you teach the Negro that he has accomplished as much good as any other race he will aspire to equality and justice without regard to race. Such an effort would upset the program of the oppressor in Africa and America. Play up before the Negro, then, his crimes and shortcomings...Lead the Negro to detest the man of African blood—to hate himself. The oppressor then may conquer, exploit, oppress and even annihilate the Negro by segregation without fear or trembling. With the truth hidden there will be little expression of thought to the contrary. (pp. 192-3)

Yet, the American African has, in large parts of the population, maintained a certain level of fear and "disinterest" in thinking beyond the boundaries of their own oppression. In the relatively few groups that have risen and fallen throughout this experience of oppression, there have been glimmers of hope that would reach certain individuals and families. This hope would assist them to do better often by refining their understanding of their situation and by shifting their identities from an oppressed and helpless individual to a "free" thinking and capable human being. These groups are often scorned and even attacked by society as being negatively "militant," reverse-racists, or trouble making religious fanatics that the "intelligent" citizen should avoid at all costs.

In reality, many of these groups challenge the "abundance of information which others have made accessible to [them]..." (p. 193). They also challenge the reality and notion that the American African is "the most docile and tractable people on earth..." (p. 193). These groups tend to be the ones who will challenge the ongoing trans-generational decadence and low expectation, poor self-concept, and inaction displayed by some American Africans. They see themselves as continuing the legacy of the "maroons" and freedom fighters that resisted enslavement, colonialism, injustice and oppression at all costs. In each of these groups, there is almost guaranteed to be a sort of re-education process designed to shake off the mental chains of distorted self-concepts.

Nonetheless:

> The mis-educated Negro joins the opposition with the objection that the study of the Negro keeps alive questions which should be forgotten. The Negro should cease to remember that he was once held a slave, that he has been oppressed, and even that he is a Negro... but this very attitude shows ignorance of the past and a slavish dependence upon the enemy to serve those whom he would destroy. The Negro can be made proud of his past only by approaching it scientifically himself and giving his own story to the world. What others have written about the Negro during the last three centuries has been mainly for the purpose of bringing him where he is today and holding him there. (p. 194)

In all of creation there is a built-in self-preservation mechanism. This natural defense can be: a tough exoskeleton or outer skin, the ability to camouflage and change colors to match the environment, the possession of claws, fangs, venom, superior physical strength and agility, swiftness, flight, the ability to produce a loud sound, the emission of foul smells, bright colors designed to warn, thorns, movements in large numbers, the ability to build weapons, tools and shelters, or growth in obscure and hard to reach places.

The amazing thing about this list is that the human being is capable of manifesting each of these defenses to one degree or another. What does it mean then, when a human being abandon's all sense of self-preservation (ingesting harmful agents, participation and promoting risky behaviors, etc.), and instead becomes the main operator in its own destruction? Psychologically speaking, this would be an indication of an underlying pathology that leads to the slow and passive-aggressive suicide. Similar to the cognitive-behavior therapeutic approach to bringing one out of the suicidal state, the aforementioned scientific approach to self-knowledge would assist in shifting one's maladaptive beliefs about themselves and their situations, and hopefully give them a new and healthy outlook on life.

The key is to center this task on information pertaining to the empowerment of the individual and the development of knowledge and skills that are directly and practically applicable. The remedy will simultaneously attack the faulty identity and the sense of learned hopelessness brought about by their trans-generational experience with oppression. Additionally, the issue of meeting basic needs must be rectified early in the process, in order to extinguish the power of external manipulation via the use of primary reinforcers (i.e., the provision of food, clothing and shelter or the promise thereof). While the oppressed maintains the ideology and value system of the oppressor, it is also important to develop a method for securing secondary reinforcers (i.e., money and other resources used to secure the primary reinforcers). The existence of negative and detrimental habits will also have to be addressed early in this process, in order to improve upon existing and prevent further health issues (i.e., alcohol and drug use, dietary habits, etc.).

In regards to the study of history and politics of one's ancestry, this author posits that this must be done for the sole purpose of understanding the development of systems that have proven effective and successful at cultivating healthy and viable people. Underlying every great and harmonious civilization is a culture that develops great and harmonious people. In regards to the general African culture, there is always a golden thread of intentional spiritual development that precipitated the growth and continued success of those societies. It is here that time would be best spent. Not only in the intellectual search for such information but the practical application of these principles in the construction of new and modernly relevant systems of human development and cultivation.

Unfortunately, many Africans and other civilizations world-wide have been forced to accept the perspective of their conquerors and have rarely successfully restored their pre-encounter worldviews. This is detrimental in the following ways: 1) the newly adopted perspective of the conqueror is usually one that degrades the value of the conquered; 2) it is usually designed to maintain the power of the conqueror over the conquered; 3) it also serves to make the conquered compliant and complacent in their own continued oppression; and 4) it decreases the likelihood that the oppressed will ever advance to the point of being able to apply deep thought to their situation and develop solutions for their ailment, rendering them perpetually dependent.

> The Negro needs to become angry with himself because he has not handled his own affairs wisely...He must not remain content with taking over what others set aside for him and then come in the guise of friends to subject even that limited information to further misinterpretation. (p. 197)

Hence, the emphasis on being able to think for one's self. To think for another, you may provide them with a singular idea; but to teach another to think for his or her self is to arm them with the power to recognize and create solutions to any problem they may encounter.

Chapter 19

Sticks and Stones...
(Appendix: Much Ado About a Name)

"They say we N-I- double G –E-R we are much more, but still we choose to ignore the obvious, man this history don't acknowledge us; we was scholars long before colleges. They say we N-I- double G –E-R we are much more, but still we choose to ignore the obvious, we are the slave and the master, what you looking for, you the question and the answer."

Nas
Nigger

"<u>N</u>*ever* <u>I</u>*gnorant* <u>G</u>*etting* <u>G</u>*oals* <u>A</u>*ccomplished"*

Tupac Shakur
Words of Wisdom

"You can only be destroyed by believing that you really are what the White world calls a Nigger."

James Baldwin
Letter to his nephew

The question of a name is more a question about identity. For what a person is called, and perhaps more importantly what they answer to, provides insight into what they are identifying with, even if only for that moment. With this said, how is one impacted by the directing of negatively defined labels such as Nigga, Bitch, Hoe, Dog, etc.; or even those labels that are not necessarily negatively defined, but that carry a meaning of inferiority in reference to some other object, person or group (i.e., minority, baby, baby boy, lil' mama, boy, girl, etc.). When dealing with the question of a name from this perspective, it becomes obvious why there would be much ado about something seemingly so simple. Amongst those scholars who write about African descendants, you will find a plethora of labels used to identify the subject of the scholarship, each carrying their own line of reasoning. For example, this author chose to use the term "American African" as opposed to the more popular version of "African American" in reference to those African descendants that currently reside in the United States. It's similar to how a box of crayons will label a blue crayon, with green accents "green-blue"; it more accurately illustrates how the African aspect of the person is at the core, and the American part is the externally applied culture. The real irony is that both the word American and the word African are derivatives of a European's name (Americus Vespucci and Leo Africanus [Grenada born and Moroccan raised], respectively.

In Woodson's era, it made sense for him and others to be concerned with the amount of energy being spent debating "if" and "what" identifying labels should be used for American Africans and their institutions. It also makes sense that there would be a willingness by others to unapologetically commit large amounts of energy to the same. Coming fresh out of plantation and reconstruction era politics and social systems, the American African still had a long way to go in the process of restating and reclaiming, for themselves, a position in society and the universe as a whole. They were still in the process of peeling back the layers of dehumanizing experiences that had taken place for hundreds of years, and was far from over in the 1930s. As stated in the Book of Genesis, man was given dominion over all things which also afforded them the power to name that which was being ruled. As a movement

towards kujichagulia (self determination), the newly freed
American African took up the challenge.

As time progressed, it became much more apparent that
the naming process was of the utmost importance because,
as stated above, it defined the identity of those being named,
which in turn constructed the personality of the people
adopting and answering to the call. Proverbs 18:21 states that
"Death and Life are in the power of the tongue..." in the case
of the American African, that power has yet to be overstood
and wielded for their own benefit. This power is embedded
in the fact that a person's life path will literally be taken on
a journey that is very much determined by how they identify
themselves; this is a point that cannot be overstated. For a
person who believes they are destined for greatness will tend to
do great things; those who believe they are worthless will tend
to do wayward and careless things.

In many indigenous societies around the world, children
are actually named based on their previously determined life
purpose. This life purpose is usually found by some process
of divination (which is an age-old practice of communicating
with one's higher spiritual power, i.e, God, Angels, Neteru,
Orisha, Ancestors, etc.) through a specified set of symbols that
have been studied and understood by an initiated (priestly)
class within the community. Based on the outcomes of this
divination, a person's destiny or life purpose is made plain,
then translated and encapsulated in what we now know to be
a name. Through this name, the person is forever reminded of
their life purpose, dispositions, strengths and challenges within
their projected walk through life. The people around them in
their community, by knowing their name, are equally made
aware of the individual's walk, and can assist them accordingly
through an interdependent and tightly woven network of
mutual accountability.

To make it plain, a person who has a destiny that involves leadership, decision making, learning amongst the wise ones, community building and the establishment and maintenance of systems of truth & justice, will carry a name such as MenaqAmurr Neferkhar, which loosely translates into "the patient and receptive Brother who grows ever more stable in what is correct (righteousness), while taking his seat amongst the great ones." Constantly, all day, every day, this individual is reminded of the lofty role they have agreed to play in society and the large amount of refinement that they must undergo to begin to approach such a destiny. They are also held accountable by those who know this name and the meaning/purpose it illustrates. Furthermore, there is usually a naming ceremony, during which this person and their name are introduced to the community with counsel being provided by the initiated class governing the event.

Many of the world's cultures adhere to a similar process and place an equal amount of emphasis on this process due to the known importance of a name and its impact on the life path of the individual. This author has experienced several times a change in name (both legally and spiritually). As a child, the author was born a junior (Jr.), carrying the same first and last name of his biological father. At around five years of age, the author's mother changed his last name to match that of her own. The intentional reasons are unknown to the author, however, the spiritual outcome and life path altering that occurred as a result is absolutely clear and without question.

This simple gesture of changing the name that a child answers to and identifies with and through, is perhaps one of the most important aspects of the developmental psychology of a human being. It shapes the role they will most likely model while also expanding or contracting their perceived possibilities in life. So what of the individual that has adopted the label of "nigga" and its accompanying personality characteristics and identifiable culture? What of the female who truly believes that the term "bitch" is indeed a term of endearment and not the label used to define a female dog? What of those who identify as minorities, and who receive special "rewards" for this identification (i.e., minority scholarships, minority grants, minority-based tax breaks, etc.), or for those like the main character in John Singleton's *Babyboy* who live a life of perpetual childhood, due to the environmental circumstances and the labels that they have adopted and from which they construct their self-image?

The recent challenge issued by Dr. William (Bill) H. Cosby to the American African community regarding the names that are given to children was partially due to his understanding of how a name can impact a person's opportunities in life; not only by how it causes them to see their own self, but also how it causes others to become biased and prejudiced towards them. This process is very complex and has several psychological underpinnings, many of which go well beyond the scope of this book. Nonetheless, it is of the highest importance that those labels and identifying markers (names) that we are able to control and influence, be controlled and influenced towards a positive outcome. This means that all negatively associated labels be discarded, not manipulated into other similarly sounding words (i.e., "ninja" instead of "nigga") and without rationalizing that it is truly a term of endearment (as many attempt to do with the words "nigga" and "bitch").

A striking example of such an attempt to rationalize away the hatred associated with such labels are found in the opening quote by Tupac Shakur where he cleverly makes an acronym for the word "nigga," turning it into a positive affirmation. Granted the person Tupac Shakur was far from ignorant and accomplished many goals in his relatively short life, the character 2Pac that he was better known for, was at times the epitome of ignorance and negative life challenges leading to his eventual assassination.

To minimize and negate the power of a name over an individual is to portray one's ignorance to the spiritual science that governs life. There is a saying that "a rose by any other name is still a rose." This statement is absolute truth and cannot be successfully argued against. It is the implied truth that is oft times flawed in its interpretation. If in fact a plant/person is what it is and cannot be directly changed merely by a label under which it is presented, then by its labeling will others approach, handle and value or devalue this thing. For example, a rose is known to usually come with thorns. Suppose a person tells another that "here is a bag of tulips," after which the unsuspecting person reaches in expecting to grab stems of beautifully scented flowers, only to get a handful of thorns along with some beautifully scented flowers. In the case where the person was told that they were grabbing into a bag of roses, and if the person indeed knows what roses are, then they are likely to have been more careful in their endeavor, in order to avoid the pain of a thorn prick.

The same goes with persons and the names and labels they choose and/or are forced to identify with. In the classic film *Roots* by Alex Haley, there is a famous scene where the main character Kunta Kente (played by LeVar Burton), under extreme threat and pain, attempts to maintain his identity as Kunta Kente, a Mandinkan Gambian from West Africa. After several days of pain and torture, his spirit is eventually broken to the degree where he will no longer fight to keep his African name, and would openly declare his new, plantation appointed name of Tobey. This scene is a clear illustration of how powerful a name is to certain individuals; and because he fought to keep the identity of his ancestry, his personality didn't immediately crumble nor did he immediately conform to the harsh plantation environment that he was now imprisoned by. A more recent example is found in the movie *Besouro* (entitled *The Assailant* in the English market), which is a movie about the capoeria-laced revolution that took place against the Portuguese colonizers in Brazil. In the opening and closing scenes, a young child walks with an elder and is told that he must choose his name based on his characteristics and attributes. Throughout the film, Besouro becomes legendary based on his knowledge of spiritual power and the adherence to his "chosen" name.

The old childhood saying that "sticks and stones may break my bones but words will never hurt me" serves the purpose of helping children to avoid super-sensitive and vulnerable reactions to the sometimes mean words directed towards them; however, it is highly misleading in regards to the power and impact that words have on all of creation. When the power of verbalizing words is coupled with the powerful vibrations, harmonies, and melodies of music, the ability to influence has become exponentially increased. In the year 2012, many are gaining very important aspects of their identities and personality traits from popular culture and music; adopting the labels, habits, cultural nuances, language use, etc., from paid actors, whose script is highly laced with elements designed to mislead and mis-educate the consumer. The impact on identity and personality is at the core of the mis-education process and is what dumbing down is all about, and is what has been communicated in various ways in the previous chapters.

If nothing else has been gained from this and Dr. Woodson's work, please endeavor to comprehend on a deeper level how susceptible the unwitting sleepwalker is to the influences of those who seek to profit from their ignorance and vulnerability. Seek to comprehend how one can truly build their own identity; an identity that is empowering and unyielding to the slick and subtle influences projected by systems of mis-education and dumbing down.

Simply ask yourself why you do what you do, why you like what you like, why you dislike what you dislike…ask yourself why you respond to certain people, situations, circumstances in the manner that you do…ask yourself what are the things in your life that cause pain and actually dis-empower your life, hindering your ability to set and reach your goals. Ask why you have the goals that you have…After asking these and other questions like them, seek the answers with an openness and receptivity to be guided by the truth. As the answers begin to make themselves apparent, cultivate the strength needed to break the patterns of dumbed down thought, speech, and/or actions, and seek to eliminate all aspects of mis-education in your life.

INDEX

D

E

F

G

H

I

J

R

S

ABOUT THE AUTHOR

Jeffery Menzise is a doctor of clinical psychology, a licensed school psychologist, researcher and college professor. He is a member of St. Johns Lodge #3, Prince White Chapter #1, and King Solomon Consistory #20 , all in Cincinnati, Ohio.

He has been initiated into the priesthood of several African-centered spiritual traditions, both on the continent of Africa and in the United States. He has also been ordained as an inter-faith, inter-denominational minister. He has authored/co-authored several articles and chapters in books, journals and on-line publications and is currently working on several children's books, mind enhancement systems, and a relationship manual.

As an accomplished and well sought after radio talk show host, relationship expert, clinician, consultant, life coach and trainer, Dr. Menzise has impacted many lives internationally. He conducts clinical trainings, parenting courses, relationship/couples retreats, relationship enhancement workshops, and serves as host to a variety of workshops and seminars for other presenters to showcase their gifts, talents, and services.

He is currently available for consultations and lectures.

Dumbin' Down

CPSIA information can be obtained at www.ICGtesting.com
Printed in the USA
BVOW02s1248130114

341515BV00005B/10/P